Children, Teachers and Learning Series

Series Editor: Cedric Cullingford

The Role of I.T.

Titles in the *Children, Teachers and Learning* series:

J. Backhouse, L. Haggarty, S. Pirie and J. Stratton *Improving the Learning of Mathematics*

M. Bonnett *Children's Thinking*

J. Campion *Working with Vulnerable Young Children*

C. Cullingford *Children and Society*

C. Cullingford *The Inner World of the School*

C. Cullingford *The Nature of Learning*

K. Gentle *Teaching Painting in the Primary School*

J. Glover and S. Ward *Children's Music*

D. Hartley *Understanding the Nursery School*

T. Jarvis *Children and Primary Science*

R. Jones *The Child–School Interface*

B. Mayall *Negotiating Health*

R. Stevenson and J. Palmer *Learning: Principles, Processes and Practices*

P. Wiegand *Children and Primary Geography*

J. Wilson and B. Cowell *Children and Discipline*

L. Winkley *Emotional Problems in Children and Young People*

The Role of I.T.

Practical Issues for the Primary Teacher

Avril Loveless

CASSELL

Cassell
Wellington House
125 Strand
London WC2R 0BB

370 Lexington Avenue
New York
NY 10017–6550

First published 1995
Reprinted 1998, 1999

British Library Cataloguing in Publication Data
A catalogue record for this book is available from the British Library.

ISBN 0-304-33214-3 (hardback)
     0-304-33217-8 (paperback)

Typeset by Action Typesetting Ltd, Northgate Street, Gloucester
Printed and bound in Great Britain by
Biddles Ltd, Guildford and King's Lynn

Contents

Foreword vii

Acknowledgements..x

Introduction...xi

1 Questions for Teachers: Why IT?......................................1

2 Communicating Information 23

3 Handling Information...51

4 Using IT to Model, Control and Monitor the World 69

5 IT for All: Empowerment and Limitations 92

6 Preparation, Planning and Review 119

7 The Role of IT in the Primary Classroom......................143

Appendix: Keeping Up to Date 161

Bibliography..164

Name Index 176

Subject Index 178

Foreword

The books in this series stem from the conviction that all those who are concerned with education should have a deep interest in the nature of children's learning. Teaching and policy decisions ultimately depend on an understanding of individual personalities accumulated through experience, observation and research. Too often in recent years decisions on the management of education have had little to do with the realities of children's lives, and too often the interest shown in the performance of teachers, or in the content of the curric-ulum, has not been balanced by an interest in how children respond to either. The books in this series are based on the conviction that children are not fundamentally different from adults, and that we understand ourselves better by our insight into the nature of children.

The books are designed to appeal to *all* those who are interested in education and who take it as axiomatic that anyone concerned with human nature, culture or the future of civilization is interested in education – in the individual process of learning, as well as what can be done to help it. While each book draws on recent findings in research and is aware of the latest developments in policy, each is written in a style that is clear, readable and free from jargon that has undermined much scholarly writing, especially in such a relatively new field of study.

Although the audience to be addressed includes all those concerned with education, the most important section of the audience is made up of professional teachers, the teachers who continue to learn and grow and who need both support and stimulation. Teachers are very busy people, whose energies are taken up in coping with difficult circumstances. They deserve material that is stimulating, useful and free of jargon and that is in tune with the practical realities of classrooms.

Each book is based on the principle that the study of

education is a discipline in its own right. There was a time when the study of the principles of learning and the individual's response to his or her environment was a collection of parts of other disciplines – history, philosophy, linguistics, sociology and psychology. That time is assumed to be over and the books address those who are interested in the study of children and how they respond to their environment.

Each book is written both to enlighten the readers and to offer practical help to develop their understanding. They therefore not only contain accounts of what we understand about children, but also illuminate these accounts by a series of examples, based on observation of practice. These examples are designed not as a series of rigid steps to be followed, but to show the realities on which the insights are based.

Most people, even educational researchers, agree that research on children's learning has been most disappointing, even when it has not been completely missing. Apart from the general lack of a 'scholarly' educational tradition, the inadequacies of such study come about because of the fear of approaching such a complex area as children's inner lives. Instead of answering curiosity with observation, much education research has attempted to reduce the problem to simplistic solutions, by isolating a particular hypothesis and trying to improve it, or by trying to focus on what is easy and 'empirical'. These books try to clarify the real complexities of the problem, and are willing to be speculative.

The real disappointment with educational research, however, is that it is rarely read or used. The people most at home with children are often unaware that helpful insights can be offered to them. The study of children and the understanding that comes from self-knowledge are too important to be left to obscurity. In the broad sense real 'research' is carried out by all those engaged in the task of teaching or bringing up children.

All the books share a conviction that the inner worlds of children repay close attention, and that much subsequent behaviour and attitudes depend upon the early years. They also share the conviction that children's natures are not markedly different from those of adults, even if they are more honest about themselves. The process of learning is reviewed as the individual's close and idiosyncratic involvement in events, rather than the passive reception of, and processing of, information.

Cedric Cullingford

Acknowledgements

This book is dedicated to Geoff Simkins with thanks for his support and encouragement.

I would like to thank the students and my colleagues in the School of Education, University of Brighton and the children and teachers in the schools in which I have worked.

Introduction

In my experience as a teacher and lecturer involved in the use of IT (information technology) in primary education I have been acutely aware of the needs of the teachers and students with whom I have been working. The emotions and attitudes relating to using IT in the classroom range from excitement and enthusiasm to fear and loathing. There has been a tremendous task of differentiation to provide experiences to encourage and challenge teachers – reassuring them whilst trying to become familiar with new technology and discussing the reasons why they might consider using IT to support children's learning and their own professional teaching and administration.

It is this range of types of knowledge – an understanding of the rationale for using IT to support learning and teaching as well as practical and technical abilities – that creates the challenge for developing children's IT capability. This capability is far more than being able to apply a variety of skills with computers. IT plays an important role in children's day-to-day lives and in the society in which they live. The skills needed to use the technology change quickly, hold few fears for most children and will soon be a commonplace part of our lives at home and school.

Research seems to indicate that IT has not had the widespread effect in classrooms that was hoped. The difference in the quality of experience in using IT seems to be related to the understanding that the teachers have about the nature of the ways in which children learn and the nature of the area of the curriculum which is being addressed. Putting word processors on every child's desk will not necessarily make children into good writers, just as putting a graphics package into every office does not produce good design. There needs to be an interplay between an understanding of the *goals* of the activity and the *variety of ways in which pupils learn*, through exploration, consultation, collaboration, guidance, questioning and explanation.

It is not possible to consider the use of IT in classrooms without reflecting upon one's beliefs about learning and teaching. IT capability can be seen as much more to do with an approach to ways of learning and working than as the development of a set of skills. Developing this understanding within the classroom will strengthen the context in which IT is used, thus strengthening the connections between the use of IT in school and the use of IT in the world outside. As Seymour Papert commented, 'Anyone who can draw as many people into situations related to learning as ... Lego or Nintendo knows something that educators who have trouble holding the attention of thirty children for forty minutes ought to want to learn' (Papert, 1993, p. 87).

CHAPTER 1
Questions for Teachers: Why IT?

Teachers need to ask themselves some important questions about the reasons for using IT in the classroom. The demands upon a teacher in a busy classroom are both educational and practical: how do children learn, what should they learn and how can this be organized effectively for all the individuals in that class? The ways in which we plan, organize and manage activities in the classroom reflect our beliefs about and aims for the children's learning. We strive to engage the children's interest, build on their motivation, encourage them to develop their successes and move forward with their difficulties. We try to help them make connections between familiar knowledge and new knowledge and urge them to develop confidence and autonomy in learning. We plan a range of activities in order to provide a variety of experiences – cognitive, social, spiritual and physical.

In short, teachers are busy people with tremendous responsibilities to the children in their care. They must have a clear view of the purpose of what they do, a clear understanding of the reasons behind what goes on in the classroom, and a clear sense of reflection upon and evaluation of the children's experiences. It is therefore important that IT (information technology) is considered in terms of the educational and practical concerns of the teacher.

IT is considered by many teachers to have great potential in the classroom, supporting both the children's learning and the work of the teacher. It is seen as something to be taken seriously in children's education, but there is also considerable uncertainty and lack of confidence in actually using it effectively. Both experienced and student teachers have expressed positive attitudes to the use of computers in schools. A survey of attitudes carried out by Jean and Geoffrey Underwood indicated that 'positive responses were received four times as often as negative responses' (Underwood and Underwood, 1990, p. 16). Another survey of student teachers' attitude to IT on entry to their

1

course also indicated that they held strong views about its importance in education. Nearly 40 per cent strongly agreed that IT was an important part of teacher education and only 5 per cent disagreed (Davis and Coles, in press).

There are, however, a significant number of teachers who do not feel confident with new technologies and their own use of them in the classroom. A national survey revealed that only 14 per cent of experienced teachers perceived themselves as competent in technology and less than 20 per cent felt able to add to a database or use graphics to present work or to develop ideas (Bennett *et al.*, 1992). There are still many classrooms in which work with the computer is seen as an 'extra', rather than an integrated part of the children's experience, and some where the computer is not even switched on.

IT can be seen to be difficult or threatening to many people for many reasons, ranging from anxiety about acquiring new skills to strongly held views about the educational worth of the activities themselves. In trying to support and encourage teachers in an area which they feel to be of great potential and yet threatening, it is important to pay attention to these questions of *why* we think IT is important and *what challenges* that brings to teachers.

Why do we need to consider using IT in education?

If education is about learning – cognitive, social, emotional, spiritual, moral and physical – then teachers must consider the best experiences, resources and environments in which this can be supported. They must also be aware of the experiences that children have outside the classroom which contribute to or constrain the quality of their learning and development. There are bold claims made for the potential of IT to enhance cognitive learning, develop problem-solving and higher-level thinking skills, and extend physical and mental abilities as a new tool used in new ways. The teacher has also to think about the ways in which IT affects the children at a practical and social level – from appliances in the home and games entertainment to virtual reality and communication with computer users on the other side of the world.

WHAT IMPACT DOES IT HAVE ON THE CHILDREN'S LIFE OUTSIDE SCHOOL?

The children arrive in the classroom having encountered and used new technologies in many aspects of their everyday lives. They will have seen money issued from cash machines; watched pricing and stock-control at the supermarket checkout; played with computer games on their own and with their friends; and been involved in interactive entertainments involving visual images and sound. With the rapid development of the home market for IT in entertainment and education – unimaginatively called by the portmanteau word 'edutainment' – some children may have had access to sophisticated technology which enables them to interact with and browse through vast amounts of information. They may have 'talking books' in which the pictures are animated and the text is read to them as required. They may have the equivalent of a full set of encyclopaedias or examples of paintings in London's National Gallery on a CD ROM disc. They may have had the opportunity to look at that information and incorporate it into their own work to include text, pictures, sound and animation. The children will arrive at school with an ease and familiarity with IT and a confident and curious approach to new technology and the skills required to help them explore. What they may need from the teacher is support in developing these skills in order to use all the information available to them creatively and effectively.

The society in which we live has undergone rapid and widespread technological change, a 'technological revolution', similar in impact to the agrarian and industrial revolutions (Toffler, 1981). IT permeates work, leisure, learning and home life. The changes have come about quickly and have affected people both in the practical ways in which they live their lives and in the cultural ways in which they see and relate to each other.

These changes to practical life can be beneficial to many people and also raise questions about the underlying values of the societies in which they are being developed. Microchip technology has become cheap and accessible to some people very swiftly, widening the gap between the 'haves' and the 'havenots' in societies and the global community. Some have access

3

to a variety of labour-saving devices, methods of information storage and retrieval and communications networks, which then affect the economic and social lives of others. Access to the communication facilities of IT can cross traditional boundaries and open up new possibilities. It is worth pondering the issues raised by the contrast between the scenario of people communicating quickly and cheaply with others for social, educational or economic development, and that of a peasant in Sudan being able to buy a wrist device showing commodity prices in New York more cheaply than he or she could buy a bag of rice making up that commodity market.

Technological revolutions are associated with shifts in patterns of employment, social change in practical living conditions, altered structures of economic and social life, and movements in social attitudes and values. Although there are those who consider this revolution to be a positive progression in society, providing powerful tools to enhance our lives, there are also many who would consider the possible consequences for social, economic, cultural and political life and would question the values of those controlling the technology.

There are also cultural changes associated with the development of IT in our wider society, in the images and expectations of technology that people hold. There can often be wide gaps between people's expectations of what IT can do and the practicalities of the actual equipment and the ways in which it is used. Problems arising from computer malfunction and human misuse pose ethical dilemmas, described clearly and often amusingly by Forester and Morrison (1990). They discuss the issues of computer crime, software theft, hacking and viruses, the invasion of privacy, artificial intelligence and the effects of computers on the quality of working life, from productivity to health and safety. People often ascribe an authority to computer systems which is unwarranted – they can be unreliable, unpredictable and limiting in the way they allow the users to organize and present information. There are legendary computer crimes where the systems of banks, insurance companies and national defence organizations have been infiltrated. There is a question about whether hackers are thieves or trespassers, criminals or 'latterday Robin Hoods' and the havoc that malignant viruses can wreak on the systems of the innocent is well known. There are also concerns about the invasion of privacy and a 'surveillance society', from personalized junk mail to the Data Protection Act, and the effects that IT will have in the workplace – replacing human workers, altering the nature and location of different types of work, and posing possible health risks such as repetitive strain injury (RSI).

The ways in which human beings view themselves in terms of their identity and potential are influenced by their beliefs about the nature of intelligence and the distinction between what is 'human' and what is 'artificial'. This is not only a discussion between 'academics', but also an issue in popular culture. There is a longstanding debate between those who think that computers will never be 'humanly intelligent' and those who see intelligence in computers developing to a stage where they will eventually 'keep us as pets'. Although this debate is continuing in universities and research institutes, whether or not computers can *actually* be intelligent does not affect the ways in which images of computers and technology are developing in our culture. Sherry Turkle's thoughtful book *The Second Self* (1984) discussed how people, from children to computer programmers, viewed the machine as 'psychological', with a sense of will and purpose. They also made links between the language used in computer programming and the models they had of their own thought and behaviour, with phrases such as 'reprogram, debug, input and memory overload' being used as jargon or slang to describe human actions or thought processes.

The distinctions between human minds and machines can become unclear in images of popular culture, exemplified by robots, the Daleks, Robocop and Terminator, with intelligence being dehumanized. Brian Matthews (1992) has argued that there is a philosophical and ideological debate about the understanding of information technology in society: computers can be seen as intelligent, useful and neutral tools, or as controlled by powerful people for surveillance, or as an ideological attempt to encourage people to think of themselves as machines and be more easily controlled. We often belittle the range of our own everyday intelligence, giving honour to those with good memories and concentration. The chess world

5

shivered when Gary Kasparov, the greatest living chess player, was beaten by a computer. The computer's large database and 'brute force' calculations were considered to represent intelligence, reflecting the feats of memory and prediction required of a human player. Curiously, people are often not aware of the tremendous information-processing feats required of the human brain in just moving around the room doing mundane tasks. It is notoriously difficult to program a 'robot butler' to choose and bring a plate of biscuits, offer them round, recognize those same biscuits if they fall on the floor and break into crumbs, and go off to find a dustpan and brush to clear up the mess.

The children therefore enter the classroom not only having used IT themselves in some way, but also being part of a society influenced by images of and anxieties about new technology. It is thus important that teachers are 'technologically literate', not only in terms of skills, but also in the understanding of the non-neutral, cultural nature of technology and the ways in which it influences what children do in schools (the curriculum) and how teachers get them to do it (pedagogy).

DOES IT SUPPORT CHILDREN'S LEARNING?

As well as asking how IT affects children in their daily lives outside the classroom, teachers should examine the claims that IT contributes to children's learning, both in and out of the classroom. There are many who claim that IT has the potential not only to support the current curriculum, but also to enhance the experience and understanding of that curriculum and even extend thinking and learning in new ways.

Of course, these claims do not assert that children placed in front of a computer will automatically learn more effectively across the curriculum. Indeed, there is evidence to suggest that, for a variety of reasons, computers in classrooms have had a disappointingly limited effect so far, despite the funding given to provide equipment in schools (Watson, 1993). There are, however, observed positive effects on children's learning with IT when the complex interactions between individual learners, their working partners, the IT resources, the teacher and the nature of the task are understood and evaluated. Effective learning takes place in a context which has interest, relevance and purpose, and it is worth exploring the characteristics of IT which can contribute to creating an engaging learning environment for children. What are computers good at that enables us to extend our thinking abilities, just as we would use tools such as scissors, trowels, knives and forks to extend our physical abilities?

A key characteristic which underlies the motivation and engagement observed in children using IT is interaction. The learner is engaged by immediate – and apparently patient – feedback, which provides the opportunity to try out different possibilities, see the consequences of decisions and actions, and plan the next moves accordingly. This could be experienced in a variety of situations using IT: playing a game and moving to different levels of difficulty, trying to compose a letter using a word processor, asking for information from a database to test a hypothesis about the best treatment for conkers, or trying to land an aircraft using a flight simulator. The feedback provided by the program about the effects of certain responses, phrases or questions offers marvellous opportunities for learning through trial and error, and safely – both physically and psychologically. This facility for interaction also allows great flexibility in the design of IT resources, which can take account of the choices and responses of invidual learners and develop the activities to meet their needs, interests and abilities. Of course, one still has to ask whether the children are being motivated in experiences which are worthwhile and desirable. There are many people concerned about the growth and accessibility of computer pornography, for example, which uses the same features of presentation and interaction for different purposes.

The ability of computers to store, organize, manipulate, send and present large amounts of data at great speed far exceeds that of human minds. This data could be numbers, text, graphics, sound and, perhaps by the time this chapter is being read, touch and smell. The computer does the 'donkey work' in processing all this data in order to provide information to be interpreted and analysed by the human user. IT can therefore take on the chores of dealing with large volumes of data with great speed, in order to free the children to think about the

7

implications of the information with which they are dealing.

The facility of IT to store, organize and retrieve large amounts of information provides the learner with a rich resource and a wide-ranging knowledge base. Children can have access to resources not necessarily available to their physical grasp in an ordinary classroom or school library, such as pictures of artefacts from museums around the world, newspaper archives, recorded speech or moving films. Multimedia information can be provided on CD ROM on subjects ranging from the Anglo-Saxons to karaoke Shakespeare; remote documents and databases can be made available across the international networks of computers, and electronic communications can be set up between interested parties around the globe – playtime groups conversing with professors.

Access to this information is much the same as access to library resources, and similar information-handling skills of browsing, making connections and evaluating are required. It is the interactive and participative nature of these resources which has the potential for creative involvement with this information. The children will be able to manage information by searching and exploring, making connections between familiar and new areas of knowledge, and then pulling together different resources to illustrate and present their own ideas. Giving children access to information and enabling them to use it in relevant and purposeful ways allows them to develop a sense of doing serious work.

One of the exciting contributions that IT makes to the children's learning environment is the potential it has to present information in new and varied ways, involving sight, sound and movement. The visual presentation of data and relationships in the forms of graphs and charts is an obvious example of making the interpretation and analysis of information more accessible. An early example of this facility was a program called Eureka which demonstrated how the water level of a running bath would change over time given different situations, from leaving the plug out to having a person jump in. The children could control the sequence of events (such as turning on the tap, putting in the plug, putting the man in the bath, leaving the tap running) and watch the consequences of their decisions, repre-

sented both pictorially by an animated 'cartoon' and graphically by a line graph plotted to show the variations of water level
throughout the sequence. These animation and graphics facilities showed very vividly the effects of these different events,
illustrating ideas of 'rates of change' in a way which amused and
engaged the children and enabled them to 'tell the story of the
graph'.

Visual relationships can also be modelled and manipulated
on the computer screen, enabling the children to investigate
the effects of altering the colours and shapes of a textile pattern
or changing the design of a 3D object. Other relationships and
effects can be modelled in this way too, from a simple animation to show the effects on a flower of feeding it different
nutrients under different conditions (the flower thrives or wilts
and dies), to complex models which represent the effects of
various factors in such diverse systems as population structures,
levels of acid rain or political policy decisions on economic
models (with much the same outcomes as the experiment with
the flower).

Computers can also present information in terms of sound,
from 'beeps' to speech and music, and of movement – controlling motors that turn gears, levers and wheels in order to move
models and robots. Virtual reality, although clumsy at present,
aims to present information to all the senses to build up images
of artificial worlds.

The capacity of IT for interactivity and the storage, manipulation and presentation of information in various forms
provides the potential for active and experiential learning.
Where learners are engaged in activities which are challenging,
and open ended, providing a degree of control over pace,
purpose and direction, there are opportunities for the development and application of a range of cognitive abilities.

What challenges does IT present for teachers working in ordinary classrooms?

Bringing IT into a classroom provokes innovation and change.
These two words alone can produce feelings of anxiety and
threat, and the first reaction may well be to put the computer

in the corner of the room, cover it with a dust sheet and use it as a place to put the pot plants – a non-interactive classroom display. Adopting innovation and being prepared to make changes involves taking risks and moving into areas where one does not feel confident or competent. This is particularly true with IT, where teachers have to learn new technical skills as well as learn to understand their educational potential.

We therefore need to ask, as teachers with our skills and beliefs about teaching and learning, these questions:

- What is this thing called 'IT capability' that requires these changes?

- How do we approach the development of this capability across the curriculum?

- What do we bring to this situation?

- How does it affect and change us?

WHAT DOES 'IT CAPABILITY' MEAN FOR CHILDREN AND TEACHERS LOOKING TO THE TWENTY-FIRST CENTURY?

If we accept that there are economic, social, intellectual and pedagogical reasons for using IT in education, we need to think carefully about how we develop – for ourselves and for the children – an understanding of how to use IT effectively and appropriately in these contexts. We need to have more than just a technical confidence with particular types of computer and particular applications. We need to know not only *how* to use a range of IT resources, but also *why* and *when* to use them.

The rate of change in the development of hardware and software is so rapid that the most powerful computer on everyone's lips in smart society in one year is sneered at for being a very basic standard the next. The technology that our children use in the next ten years will probably be unrecognizable from the desktop boxes and keyboards of today. Computers may well be part of our body jewellery, just as the first chronometers are now worn on our wrists. What we now see on a screen may be projected onto spectacles in front of our eyes; we may communicate with the computer by speech or touch; and the computer itself may be incorporated into an earring or, given the rate of change of men's business fashion, a tie-pin.

'Computer skills' which introduce children to a set of specific techniques are limiting and soon redundant. We need to think in a broader, more timeless way about an *IT capability* which can apply understanding and competence to the general processes of dealing with information. Children need to develop and apply an understanding not only of how IT can assist them in their work for a specific task, but also of the ways in which it affects the nature of that work. They need as well to have an understanding of the ways in which the classroom activities relate to the use and impact of IT in the wider world. They may be using a word processor to present their story, but do they have insight into how that might affect the writing process itself? What are the advantages and disadvantages of using IT in a particular situation? How does it compare with other methods of working? Does it bring something new to the situation in terms of efficiency, working patterns or ways of thinking? Does IT constrain the activity in any way? How does it compare with the ways that IT is used in our wider society beyond the school and classroom?

This notion of a broad view and understanding is described as 'capability' rather than 'skill'. The words 'capable' and 'capability' carry the meanings of having power or fitness for a task, being qualified and able, being open to or susceptible to development. They imply a knowledge or skill being turned to use, an ability which is used actively, involving understanding and choice.

In the National Curriculum, IT capability is described as:

- knowledge about IT applications and about IT tools
- the skill to use appropriate IT skills effectively
- an understanding of the new opportunities IT provides
- knowledge of the effects and limitations of IT.

(NCC, 1990, A1)

It is more than the ability to use particular IT tools, such as a word processor, database, graphics package or dictionary of dinosaurs on a CD ROM. It is an understanding of the *purpose* for using such applications. Detailed knowledge of particular techniques will be learned more effectively if they are required to achieve a specific end. This is an acknowledged characteristic of meaningful learning; and yet often 'school skills' can be divorced from 'real practice'. This was clearly illustrated in the experience of a 14-year-old boy working on an art project in school, supported by an 'artist in residence' using a sophisticated multimedia IT system to develop the presentation. The boy, perceived as a disaffected low achiever, was gripped by the problem of animating his work using a complicated 'authoring package' to assemble and link his images. He could explain what he wanted to do and then use and remember every detailed technique the artist suggested, combining his new skills to develop further ideas with excitement, enthusiasm and confidence – characteristics rarely shown in his usual school work.

Of course, such 'breakthroughs' with pupils are not restricted to IT, but this illustrates how the boy's IT capability was developed through the interaction between the engagement in an activity important to him, the opportunities the IT resources provided, the support and encouragement provided by the consultant/instructor, and the confidence and challenge provided by success. IT capability is knowing when to apply or develop a particular skill in using an IT resource in order to exploit or extend a situation. Awareness of the reasons for using IT and the effect it has, both on the context and on the participants involved, is an important aspect of IT capability and one that can be transferred to new situations with new resources.

The notion of IT capability can also include a critical and confident attitude to learning with the technology. Confidence is often the key to competence, and we can adapt to new resources much more easily if we have the confidence that we know what we would like to do with those resources. If we know that we wish to produce a poster, write a novel, organize a school journey or participate in a computer chess tournament around the world, we will have a real context in which to acquire, apply and develop particular skills. Guy Claxton (1984) describes how we hold on to our beliefs in our own worth and identity by trying to maintain a degree of competence, consistence, control and comfort. Yet he argues that significant learning occurs when individuals risk not being competent, consistent, in control and comfortable, and experiment with new situations and untried ways of doing things. Innovation and change do place people in positions of anxiety and lack of confidence, but they also provide the opportunities for new learning and new competences. A confidence in one's 'IT capability' to try new skills and think about their appropriate application will provide a sound basis for exploration.

Is there an IT capability for teachers? The ideas encapsulated in 'IT capability' describe a general range of skills and understandings required by effective members of an 'information society'. Are there further requirements in an IT capability for teachers, relating to the specific demands of education, both professionally in their work with children and personally in their own administration and learning?

The National Council for Educational Technology (NCET) asked teachers, teacher educators, head teachers and inspectors to meet and discuss what might be required of student teachers as a basis for becoming practising teachers whose professional development continued through induction and in-service education. IT capability for teachers was therefore described as:

basic technical capability
- use a range of IT resources and applications with confidence
- manage IT resources
- reflect on his/her own learning of IT skills

positive attitudes to IT and its place in education
- use at least one particular IT application with a high degree of mastery
- tackle new applications without hesitation
- assess the educational potential of new technologies

understanding of the educational potential of IT
- demonstrate an understanding of the ways in which IT contributes to teaching and learning

ability to use IT effectively in the curriculum
- prepare schemes of work which integrate IT use
- plan and deliver learning activities involving the selection and use of IT appropriate to age phase and National Curriculum subject
- justify the use of IT within a particular scheme or activity

manage IT in the classroom
- use IT effectively with a small group and in a normal classroom environment

evaluate IT use
- critically review a range of software and hardware
- evaluate their usefulness and appropriateness for pupils of different ages and abilities
- appraise his/her own personal use of IT

ensure differentiation and progression
- plan and implement a scheme of work appropriate for an individual pupil which incorporates the use of IT
- effectively assess and record pupil achievement
- modify the planned scheme as necessary to ensure pupil progress.

(NCET, 1994a)

Although this list may seem daunting, the expectations are embedded in the daily practice and development of a primary-school teacher: using and becoming familiar with resources, reflecting upon the purpose for planning and preparing work, managing and evaluating activities, and learning from experience in order to provide appropriate activities for the children in the class.

The context in which teachers develop IT capability is therefore one which has two important elements, personal and professional. Personally, teachers will need to have confidence and competence in order to use IT appropriately in their own work of preparation, planning, organization, management, assessment and evaluation. They will also need to have an understanding of the ways in which children learn with IT and the implications for the art of teaching in this learning environment.

HOW DO NEW TECHNOLOGIES SUPPORT THE NATIONAL CURRICULUM IN SCHOOLS?

A model for the curriculum in England and Wales can be seen as consisting of concentric circles. The National Curriculum, with its subjects, skills, dimensions and themes, forms the centre; the basic curriculum, made up of the National Curriculum and religious education, surrounds that; and the whole curriculum – that is, the whole experience of what children learn at school, from sums to social graces – forms the outer circle. IT capability is seen not as a 'subject' but as a capability developed through and across the whole curriculum, for all ages.

In planning to use IT in the primary classroom, the teacher must consider not only how the children's IT capability is to be developed, but also how that supports the children's understanding of the curriculum area. There are therefore two important elements to be thought about in approaching the development of 'IT capability': the purpose of the activity itself and the nature and quality of the children's experience in learning. Although these are different perspectives, they combine to give a more complete picture of what is actually going on when children use IT. The fable of the three blind men described how they approached an elephant and thought they had encountered a rope, a snake and a wall by touching its tail, trunk and side – each one limited by one point of view. Teachers must be careful not to focus on just one aspect of the children's learning experiences.

How can the purpose of the activity be described? The view of IT capability in the National Curriculum focuses on the purpose of the activities which can be carried out right across the curriculum, not restricted to specific subject areas. In fact, in Key Stages (KS) 1 and 2, IT capability is clearly seen as being developed through other curriculum areas, not as a 'subject' in its own right needing extra time.

There are two main 'strands' in the primary Key Stages:

1　communicating and handling information (KS 1 and 2);

2　controlling and modelling (KS1) and controlling, monitoring and modelling (KS2).

Throughout these the children are encouraged to 'examine and discuss their experiences of IT, and look at the use of IT in the outside world.' DfE, 1995, p. 2).

Communicating and handling information focuses on children's progressive use of a variety of applications to collect, organize, store, retrieve, analyse and present information for themselves and for a range of audiences. IT can be used to originate, craft and present creative ideas in words, symbols, pictures or non-verbal sound. Information can be organized and stored in written documents, diagrams and pictures, musical compositions, databases and computer models, either set up by the children or made available on disc, on CD ROM or through communication networks. Questions and enquiries can develop which need the children to search through the stored information, analyse the findings, and present the ideas in appropriate and engaging media.

All these activities can develop in complexity and sophistication throughout the child's school career. This spiral of 'sophistication' can be seen both in the development of techniques and competence with IT resources and in the complexity of the tasks themselves. Progression is provided for the children in their IT capability and in their engagement in the curriculum task. A child in the reception class, using a word processor to write a caption and a name to go with a picture painted with a graphics program, will be doing activities of 'communicating information' similar to those of a pupil in Year 6, using a simple desktop publishing package to integrate the copy and scanned photographs provided by the 'sports journalists' group for the class newspaper. In the same way, a child using a spreadsheet to chart the comparisons between the cost of living in Victorian times and the present day is doing similar 'information-handling' activities to the child who is setting up a simple database to record the appearance and habitat of minibeasts found near the pond, in order to find out what types of creature live under stones.

Controlling, monitoring and modelling encourages the children to create instructions to control events and see the consequences of their actions in real or imaginary situations. They can give instructions to programmable toys, see the results and modify their instructions; they can use sensors to observe changing events in and outside the classroom; they can explore imaginary worlds in adventure games and see what would happen if they changed different features of a simulation. Thus a group of children solving puzzles in order to follow a quest in an imaginary rain forest, and another group building a Lego model of Big Ben which chimes when it senses that the hour hand has reached the top, are both using IT to investigate the results of their predictions and refine their decisions.

What are the nature and quality of the children's experience in learning? Another view of IT capability focuses on the learners using IT and the different types of experience that they might have, rather than the activities themselves. Kemmis *et al.* (1977) developed a useful model of the ways in which computer-assisted learning (CAL) could be described. Although their work was with students using mainframe computers in the 1970s, the focus on the types or 'paradigms' of learning that were observed still has relevance today.

The types of computer use described in the model can be grouped into four main areas:

1 *Instructional,* having its roots in programmed learning, where a task is broken down to give practice and feedback in a specific area such as number bonds or spelling. These programs were sometimes called 'drill and practice' or 'worksheets on wheels', in that they echoed many of the reinforcement tasks used in classrooms. This paradigm underlies many 'training' programs.

2 *Revelatory,* allowing guided discovery and revealing under-lying models. Simulations and adventure games typify this paradigm in that the user tries to discover the 'variables' and 'rules' by trial and error and feedback. An under-standing of the situation, whether it be real, as in the simulation of a nuclear reactor, or an imaginary adventure in a fantasy castle, is gradually built up as the designer's model is revealed.

3 *Conjectural,* encouraging playful exploration and the manipulation and testing of ideas which enable the learn-ers to set up their own models and test hypotheses. Asking the question, 'What would happen if I tried...?' puts the user in control of the activity, able to learn from the conse-quences of certain decisions which produce predicted or

unexpected outcomes. Using programming languages such as Logo, or following a series of questions in interrogating a database to test a hypothesis, are examples of the children constructing their own models and trying them out.

4 *Emancipatory*, reducing the workload and using the computer's facility to process and manipulate data at great speed, thus allowing more time for the learner to be more productive in the analysis, interpretation and presentation of information. The standard IT tools of the office, such as word processors, graphics packages and statistical presentation applications, are included in this type of software.

Classroom activities which use IT will often include more than one of these paradigms, and in planning learning experiences it can be useful to involve the children in thinking about how they are using IT in particular tasks. They can develop insights into the variety of ways of working by asking the questions:

- Am I using IT as a tool?

- Am I using IT to learn something more about a particular subject or topic?

- Am I using IT as a catalyst to help me think?

IT as a *tool* enables children and teachers to work efficiently and present information clearly; for example, using a word processor in an 'emancipatory' way to produce and print out a story.

IT as a *resource for learning* provides support in teaching and learning in the curriculum, whether reinforcing particular skills or concepts in an 'instructional' mode, or giving the opportunity for insight into the nature of the subject itself in a 'revelatory' or 'conjectural' mode. A word processor can be used to give insight into the writing process itself, drawing attention to composition, editing and redrafting, just as a simulation of planning routes for building a road can highlight issues of environmental impact in geography.

IT as a *catalyst* can help children to think in new ways by using the 'conjectural' mode to help them explore their ideas and try out new possibilities. A common example of this is using the Logo language to program a 'robot turtle' to follow a set of commands which can be combined in increasingly complex structures. Another new area for exploration is that of writing in 'hypertext', where the children can make connections between pieces of text through which the reader can choose to move along many possible routes, the narrative having the potential to be different every time, according to the choices made.

DO WE NEED TO THINK ABOUT OURSELVES AS TEACHERS IN DIFFERENT WAYS?

IT will not replace teachers, at least not effective teachers who see their role as encompassing more than being a 'knowledge base', providing input and feedback to correct responses. IT can be a catalyst, however, for thinking about one's roles and responsibilities as a teacher.

The social quality of learning, which involves communication, interaction, negotiation and sharing, was emphasized in the theoretical framework conceptualized by L. S. Vygotsky. This theory of 'teaching and learning' which drew attention to the role of language and the social, interactive nature of cognitive development, has far-reaching implications for the development of teaching skills. The understanding of the importance of the teacher being 'on the growing edge of the child's competence', as described by Jerome Bruner (1986, p. 77), is reflected in the ways in which he or she organizes and manages experiences and resources in the classroom.

Olson (1988) noted that computers affected teachers in that they rethought what they taught, their role in teaching, the methods they used, and the values underpinning their general approach to teaching and learning. A few years ago one of my colleagues arrived in an agitated state. He had been thinking about the philosophy of Seymour Papert in his work with Logo and children's mathematical thinking. 'You'll have to help me', he cried. 'I've just thrown all my text books that I've used for the last ten years into a bin bag. I'm going to start again!' It took a little time to calm him and discuss the advantages of reflecting on one's practice over time, tackling new ideas at a manage-able rate, and not throwing the baby out with the bath water – particularly not before morning playtime.

Teachers and children adopt a variety of roles in the class-room, and the ways in which we learn to balance and 'choreograph' these roles is central to the refinement of our teaching skills and the development of the children's autonomy and higher-level thinking. These roles have been observed and described by many researchers and onlookers. Eunice Fisher (1993a) described a variety of roles for teachers, from manager and leader to co-worker and facilitator. Rosemary Fraser and her colleagues reported some detailed and interesting observa-tions of the roles taken by teachers, children and computers in mathematics lessons. They noticed that, in the interaction between children and computers, there were times when the computer was in the role of manager and knowledge provider, enabling the teacher to adopt other roles, such as counsellor, fellow learner and resource. The pupils also shifted in their roles, often assuming or 'imitating' those usually taken by the computer or the teacher. 'This led them to take greater respon-sibility for the learning activity and invariably move into the higher level skill area' (Fraser *et al.*, 1988, p. 228). Elizabeth Wellburn *et al.*, (1993, p. 156) also reported a school action research project where technology acted as a catalyst for change and teachers became 'more like guides and less like sources of information'.

The unexpected nature and extent of teacher interventions with children using IT was analysed by Celia Hoyles and Ros Sutherland, working with children using Logo (1989). Although the teachers were trying not to intervene or become involved, in order to let the children solve the problems them-selves, they did, in fact, play a complex role in supporting and structuring the activity. Hoyles and Sutherland noticed that there was a sequence in which the 'teachers' would provide initial information as requested, to support and encourage pupils in their new techniques and ideas. They would then step back, take a deliberately non-interventionist stance to promote exploration and autonomy, and then return in order to make suggestions to 'stretch' the now more confident learners. The teacher therefore plays a vital role in providing appropriate structure, direction and guidance in children's learning. The 'teacher's dilemma' is described by Neil Mercer as:

> the problem of reconciling an experiental, non-didactic, 'progressive' approach to learning with the requirement that learners follow a given curriculum and do not waste their time chasing intellectual red herrings or wandering up alleys that the teacher knows full well are blind.
>
> (1993, p. 36)

In using IT in the classroom the teacher has a responsibility to provide both technical support for the operation of the resources and a quality of understanding of the field of knowledge involved in the task. The children will need a degree of initial support in selecting appropriate resources for the task, learning the techniques to use a particular application, and knowing how to save, print out and retrieve their work. In building up the children's competence and confidence with different resources, one should also involve them in discussions about the applications and effects of IT in their work, the advantages and disadvantages of using it for tasks, and how their use compares with the way it is used in the world at large. It is interesting to consider the mental models that the children have of how a computer works and what it is doing when it runs a program or saves their work. Hughes *et al.* (1987) conducted some interesting – and sometimes delightful – interviews with children, asking them how they thought the computer worked and whether it could think. Many were unclear about the first – 'a wee engine', 'a brain ticket thing' – and many also had a psychological view of the computer, attributing animistic qualities of willingness and thought.

The delicate balance between competence and understanding that characterizes IT capability often develops whilst the learner is doing something else. That is, it does not exist separately from the context in which the children are working, whether that context is helping to organize a field trip or playing an adventure game. A teacher needs to have an understanding of, and enthusiasm for, a subject as a body of knowledge with connections to other subjects, and to be able to

21

share the processes that are involved. Identifying a question for investigation in science – what makes the best paper dart, for example – could lead to the setting up of fair tests to check different variables, such as design, materials, size and strength of the thrower. These could then be recorded and stored on a database for interrogation to test the initial hypothesis. In mathematics, the development of the concept of angles and turn and the relationship between interior and exterior angles could be supported by giving instructions to a moving turtle or robot. Aspects of conferencing and redrafting in the writing process could be highlighted by drawing attention to the facilities of a word processor. In each of these three brief examples, the rationale for using IT arises from the nature of the task, not from the need to use IT.

The ImpacT Report, which was an evaluation of the impact of IT on children's achievements in primary and secondary schools, found that IT did make a contribution to learning, but that this was dependent upon a range of factors, 'the most important being that of the role of the teacher' (Watson, 1993, 1.3.2). 'Effective use of IT was supported by individual teachers' understanding of, and willingness to experiment with, the underlying philosophy of the software being considered for use by the pupils' (Watson, 1993, 7.3.2.1).

This finding can be illustrated by two cautionary tales of the children's boredom and bewilderment when their use of IT is not grounded in a purposeful starting point, question or challenge. In the first, the children spent two weeks setting up a database of ninety-nine records of Olympic event results and then asked wearily, 'What do we do with them now?' In the second, the children entered all the usual facts about 'Ourselves' into a simple database program and the teacher suggested that they used the file to find out who was the tallest child. The group obediently set about the task as instructed, apart from one who looked puzzled for a moment before turning to the teacher and saying, 'Wouldn't it be quicker if we all just lined up by the wall?' Making the connection between the art of teaching (pedagogy) and the children's experience of IT (practice) lies at the heart of the development of IT capability for teachers and children.

CHAPTER 2
Communicating Information

We communicate information to others in a variety of forms, to different audiences and for diverse purposes. We communicate through the written word, pictures, speech and music, symbols, touch and even through taste, smell and our body movements. We communicate to an audience which includes, at various times, ourselves, our loved ones, our friends and family, colleagues, bosses, those who represent us, those who provide a service to us, interest groups and the general public. We have the opportunity to communicate in different ways: in debate and demonstration, letters in the newspaper, poetry and paintings, dinner party conversations, bus-stop chat, pillow talk, personal diaries and talking to the bathroom mirror. We also communicate for different purposes: to give facts, figures and details; to maintain contact with other people in economic, social, intellectual, emotional and spiritual interaction; to share our creative expression of feelings, beliefs, interests and desires; to provoke thought, reflection and change in others and establish and maintain relationships, exchanging intimacies in tears and jokes.

What can information technology bring to this richness of human communication? A framework introduced in Chapter 1 viewed the potential of IT as a tool, a resource for learning and as a catalyst for provoking new thought. In communicating information, IT as a tool can provide a variety of media to produce an item which can be communicated and shared. As a resource for learning, it can help to provide some insight into the nature of the task, whether writing, drawing, painting, designing or composing. As a catalyst for provoking thought, it can present opportunities for looking at communication and interaction in new ways. It can also extend the audience for our communication, sending information across a network of readers, listeners and watchers around the globe. Alexander Graham Bell could not have envisaged fully that his invention of the 'telephone' for broadcasting concerts would be used for conversations between Oldham and Omaha. Neither could Charles Babbage have foreseen that his Difference Engine for making computations would develop into a system for video conferencing and chess games in cyberspace.

The widespread modes of communication with IT have, until recently, been the written word, visual images and sound. Touch and movement are being explored in robotics and virtual reality, and taste and smell are being developed for applications such as wine tasting, and soon, no doubt, will be incorporated into home and school resources. These distinctive modes are now being combined to provide 'multimedia' experiences in entertainment and education.

Throughout each of these modes of communication run common themes: composition and structure, manipulation and transformation, 'craft' in refining, editing and redrafting, and presentation. There are also advantages and disadvantages, opportunities and limitations in using IT, and it is important for teachers not only to think about the nature of the tasks themselves, but also to listen to the voices of writers, artists, musicians, designers and educators who use – and choose not to use – new technology to communicate. The following sections will explore some of these themes in relation to writing and visual images, considering the ways in which they are common and particular to the different modes and discussing how they can be developed and combined in the classroom.

Writing and IT

Why do we ask children to write and which skills do we wish them to develop in order to be confident writers? What are the elements of the writing process which we are trying to encourage in young children? What are the stategies that good writers adopt and how can poorer writers or reluctant writers be encouraged and supported? What does a teacher need to understand about the writing process in order to support young writers? How can IT support or constrain children in their confidence in and attitude to their writing? How can IT support learning about and learning through writing? How can IT highlight the complexities of the creative process of writing?

THE WRITING PROCESS

Hunter clearly identified the demands of the writing process. He used the analogy of the writing of a book to describe a 'hierarchy of concerns' which the writer must consider simultaneously (Hunter, 1988). The stroke of the pencil in handwriting, the spelling of a word, the placing of that word in a sentence, the linking of sentences to paragraphs, the contribution of the paragraph to the chapter, the place of the chapter in the structure, and the overall intention and plot of the book all lie on a continuum, encompassing themes from composition to presentation. Each level of these concerns requires the development and application of different writing skills, and many children focus on the immediate demands of spelling and handwriting, without having the opportunity to develop the higher-order skills.

Hunter suggests a number of characteristics demonstrated by good writers in balancing the whole writing process, ranging from knowledge about the subject to choosing an approach commensurate with the task. It is just as important to have the sense of a 'voice' with something to say, an awareness of the audience and a view about how to write and present the finished product appropriately as it is to have automation of some of the other skills, such as handwriting and using correct spelling, punctuation and grammar. Between the inspiration and motivation to write and the presentation of the final piece is the working with and crafting of the text. An understanding of the 'malleability' of the text and the importance of reading, reflecting, editing and redrafting that text is an essential part of the writing process, rather like the refining reflection needed in producing a piece of sculpture in wood or stone. The image of Michelangelo's unfinished *Captives* struggling to free themselves from the stone is one which exemplifies the common state of people learning the creative process, whether it be to produce an imaginative story, a poem or an assignment.

WRITING WITH NEW TECHNOLOGY

What are some of the claims made for the use of IT in children's writing? There are many who extol its virtues and the ways in which it can help children in realizing their potential as writers. It can bring them 'much closer to writing as "real" writers do' (Hunter, 1988, p. 6) and offer the children 'an opportunity to become more like adults, indeed like advanced professionals, in their relationship to their intellectual products and to themselves' (Papert, 1980, p. 31).

There are also many who would sound a note of caution, observing that the children do not always interact with the word processor as predicted or desired. They can be 'kept busy' with a writing task with fairly low-level demands and not use the potential of the word processor to help them develop their writing skills. The teacher needs to be aware of the underlying *purpose* of the writing activity in order to structure the children's experience and employ appropriate teaching strategies. The children also need to be aware of the constraints and limitations of using IT in a creative process such as writing in order to appreciate the complexities of the process and recognize and develop themselves as writers.

There are various IT resources seen to have potential to support writing, from the first marks on the page to the final publication. The word processor, the desktop publisher, hypertext tools and communication links provide facilities for the whole process of writing and presenting information. A word processor deals with the production and manipulation of text from the stage of 'making the mark' in order to spell a word, to the consideration of moving, replacing and redrafting to provide meaning and structure. The desktop publisher focuses on the presentation and arrangement of text and visual images in an appropriate form, such as a particular style of headings, formatting and pictures. Many word processors combine the two functions, organizing both text and format in the process of communicating information through writing. 'Multilingual' word processors provide a wide range of fonts to represent characters in languages from Gujerati to German; some word processors also include support in outlin-

ing and developing the structure of writing, and some provide
not only spelling checkers and a thesaurus, but grammar and
style checkers. The last of these, however, can be open to
dispute: when Conan Doyle's *The Hound of the Baskervilles* was
subjected to a 'style check', it was reported to include
sentences which were too long, contained too many clauses
and made incorrect use of the word 'that'!

MAKING MARKS AND CHECKING ACCURACY

At primary level children lurch across great expanses of unlined
paper, taking as long as two years (or even more) to achieve
adequate neuromuscular control over their recaltricant pencils. In
the meantime they are obliged to filter the richness and wonder of
their imaginative response to the world through crabbed and
convoluted script.

(Clark, 1985, p. 12)

Michael Clark describes the painful nature of much of a
child's writing experience at school. For many children the
physical effort of handwriting can get in the way of their confidence in communicating their ideas through writing. The
prospect of correcting spelling mistakes or redrafting for
clearer meaning or expression and copying out the final
version can be very daunting to any writer. Many children associate writing with the task of handwriting for neatness and
correctness, and some connect that directly with the experience of a dog-eared paper with crossings out and india-rubber
marks. As one 8-year-old child expressed it, 'I write less. Then I
have less to copy.'

The ability of a word processor to edit text at this basic level
is obvious. Learning to use the keyboard can still be slow for a
child, and it is possible to use concept keyboards, word lists
and adult 'scribes' to help when appropriate. Once the text is
entered, however, it can be seen clearly on the screen and
printed out. The process of correcting spellings and punctuation by moving the cursor, deleting the error and inserting a
correction is time-saving and does not threaten the child's
perseverance with and image of the piece of writing.

Semour Papert commented that 'For most children rewrit-
ing a text is so laborious that the first draft is the final copy,

and the skill of rereading with a critical eye is never acquired' (Papert, 1980, p. 30). The emotional effect that this could have was demonstrated vividly by the reaction of children with whom I was working in a local school. Two 7-year-old 'reluctant writers', Billy and Joe, were writing their account of the Creation on the word processor. Billy had announced that he was an 'expert' because his dad had a computer at home. He was pleased to give me an extra print out of his story, but did not wish to add his name to it: 'Oh *no*, I'll only have to write it all out again.' When I suggested that this would not be the case and that he could insert his name after the title *and* alter the initial letter to a capital he looked very seriously at his edited work, took a deep breath, frowned at the screen and said, 'Now I'm a *real* expert.' He then used his new-found skill to address some of the other points the teacher had made about his first story and tell his friend Joe how to do it. His story developed in accuracy and length as his ideas could be inserted at different points.

There are several features of word processors which can support or constrain writers in the initial drafting of text: the design of the keyboard, spelling checkers and 'reading aloud'. Many people are concerned that handwriting skills will atrophy as we use keyboards more and more. Many are also frustrated at the slowness of using a keyboard without typing skills. Some would argue that we should consider keyboard skills and handwriting as equally important in school, although the design of IT resources moves so quickly that we could soon be using voice or handwriting input to computers instead of an inefficient QWERTY keyboard. Given the current level of IT resourcing in schools it is unlikely that we could dispense with handwriting, and indeed, we should not ignore the versatility, individuality, creativity and aesthetic quality connected with calligraphy. It could be suggested that children could develop their handwriting for the final copies of their written work from the edited print outs of the work they have composed and redrafted on a word processor, thus separating out the motor from the cognitive skills of writing.

In addition to helping to 'make the marks on the page', a word processor can also check the accuracy of the letters and words. There has been much discussion of the advantages and disadvantages of using a spell checker and a thesaurus with young writers. One advantage is certainly in the support that is given, thus taking away some of the anxieties and slow progress associated with trying out spellings. Spelling checkers compare the words in the text with those in a stored dictionary and indicate any discrepancies, whether because a word is not present in that particular dictionary or because it is misspelt. Alternative spellings can be suggested, often producing modern-day howlers when out of context. The writer has still to decide whether the word is incorrectly spelt and choose an appropriate alternative or teach the dictionary a new word to be recognized in the future.

The checking can be done at intervals decided by the writer, or can be continuous, indicating unknown spellings as they are being typed in. Spelling checkers which signal a problem by a 'bleep' can hinder the flow of ideas by causing the children to be distracted and lose their thread. This was noted by Barry Smith, who felt that the technology had become 'too powerful; it was no longer a tool with which to write but the master, guiding the students in a way which was highly inappropriate' (Smith, 1993, p. 22). Certainly it is important to draw attention to the limitations to, as well as the support for, learning spelling. The suggested alternatives may well bear more relation to the actual letters than the intended meaning. This is particularly noticeable with the writing of dyslexic children, whose attempts at words are often so unrelated to the original that the spell checker makes bizarre suggestions which have no connection with the meaning and context of the surrounding text. It is possible, however, to design the facilities with the needs of the developing writers in mind, where the spelling and thesaurus dictionaries can be built up according to the knowledge and understanding of the writer.

Some word processors for children have a talking facility which attempts to read back the written text. This can be a gimmick which the children love to play with, but can also be seen as a teaching resource. The children are usually pleased to hear their work being read aloud 'by the computer', but are often delighted when the voice cannot read some of the

29

words. They realize that it cannot read as well as they can, particularly some of the difficult words with tricky and non-phonetic spelling which it has not been programmed to recognize. They enjoy trying to trick the computer by writing lists of words which are not said as they are spelt or lists of words which are easy – not to mention all the obvious words meant to shock or irritate!

Using a word processor in basic editing for accuracy provides the writer with an emancipatory model of learning. The tool enables the user to work more quickly and efficiently at 'inauthentic labour' – the donkey work – leaving more time and opportunity for critical reading and reflection. It is interesting to note that Billy in my example above was also working in a conjectural model, investigating the consequences of his actions in using the technique of deletion and insertion, learning and practising the technique in order to apply it in different situations.

It is clear that the teacher plays an important role in sharing the checking and correction of writing at this basic level of editing. It is important that a judgment is made about the appropriate number and nature of corrections to make in a child's work – appropriate to the children, their confidence in and attitude to their own writing and the level of motivation and understanding of the redrafting process. The teacher should be sensitive to the level at which the children can deal with basic editing; maintaining the balance between encouragement to refine and to improve and discouragement and lack of motivation. There should also be an awareness of particular needs of the child which may require a special focus, from a common spelling mistake to specific learning difficulties.

COMPOSING, AND REDRAFTING

Writing is difficult and needs time for rereading, reflection and refinement. Most of what we write, apart from the most hurried shopping list or note, needs some consideration after the first ideas have been composed and written down. Whether we are trying to express ourselves in a letter, poem, report, imaginative story or article, we take time to consider the phrasing, structure and 'voice' of the piece. We think about whether there might be a more appropriate word or phrase, a more efficient, elegant or evocative way of communicating our ideas through written words.

The word processor allows the writer to work on and revisit a piece of work over a period of time, and writing can be saved and retrieved at a later date for further consideration. It is easy to treat the text as malleable, editing and correcting letters and words, moving, deleting and restructuring sentences, paragraphs and sections. The writer can consider composition, manipulation and refinement of the structure of the text as well as the correct position and spelling of words. Print outs can be taken along the way to be read and discussed with a conference group, forming the basis of the redrafting task. If kept, they will show the journey that a piece of work has made from rough ideas and first draft to finished product.

This focus on composition and structure can be an exciting part of the writing process, where the child has the opportunity to 'craft' the text and work as a 'real' writer, experiencing the discussion, feedback and struggle of writing. Writers have different styles of composition, two extremes sometimes being referred to as Mozartian – an ability to compose in the head and write down a perfect and finished product – and Beethovian – an ability to write down different and disconnected ideas and then discard, redraft and connect those ideas many times before the final result is accepted (Daiute, 1985).

Children are asked to write to order many times in a primary classroom, but are often not given the time or opportunity to reflect upon and develop their ideas, thus moving on to a different level of writing and thinking about their own work and thoughts. The word processor offers the opportunity to take care of some of the basic editing problems that can hinder new writers, and can provide the tools to manipulate and develop a piece of text in ways which would have been long-winded and demotivating by traditional pencil, paper and rubber methods.

PRESENTING WRITING TO AN AUDIENCE

The appearance of our work is important if others are to look at it and read it to some purpose. It should be in an appropriate form and style, whether it be a hurried note on a fax machine, a report requiring consistent numbering of headings, a newspaper needing eye-catching headlines and column layout, or a novel structured into chapters and sections. All writers must consider these issues, and the new technology of word processors, desktop publishers and multimedia systems allows them to manipulate, experiment and refine these visual aspects of the written word.

At this level children can decide whether to use a word processor which will give them some flexibility and variety in the types of font and format that they can use. This can be as simple as choosing to use a large, bold 'jelly' font for a label to go on the pencil tin, or as sophisticated as varying the fonts and styles in a text to suit headings and paragraphs as suggested by professional designers. They will need to ask questions such as 'Where is this piece of writing going to be seen and read?' 'Who will read it?' and 'How can I attract their attention and help them to read it quickly and easily?'

The appearance and presentation of a child's writing are important, not only to the audience. Many less able writers are those whose work has always been scruffy, difficult to read and presented on aged paper which has seen many rubbings out and smudges as the time taken to compose the piece has ticked by. Being able to print work which looks 'professional' and will be relatively easy to amend and update is a tremendous boost to reluctant writers. There are many tales of children, who had before barely written a full page, working on the word processor with great concentration and over a long period of time to write a book for the book corner or their younger brothers and sisters.

COLLABORATION

Many writers have highlighted the particular contribution that a word processor can bring to encouraging collaborative writing among children (Chandler, 1984; Scrimshaw, 1993). This collaboration can extend from the brainstorming and composing stage to the conferencing, discussing and publishing of a piece of writing. It can also include feedback and discussion from the intended readers, such as the younger children or peers reading a class story book or newspaper. When a group of children is working around a computer screen, there are many opportunities for collaboration and shared work. The screen is easily seen by all the group and belongs to the whole group, unlike the piece of paper held by the appointed scribe. The keyboard operator can be chosen for his or her particular skill in typing, or the task shared between group members. Comments about ideas, corrections and manipulations to the task can be discussed, tried out and discarded after consideration. The experimentation and change required in a group activity is made easier by the word processor's editing and redrafting facilities. Work can be printed out for the whole group to consider and discuss and the writing saved for further work at a later date.

DEVELOPMENTS IN THE TECHNOLOGY: PORTABLES, ELECTRONIC MAIL AND HYPERTEXT

As advances are made in the design, power and accessibility of IT resources, interesting questions are raised for teachers thinking about the nature of the writing process with their children. For example, portable computers enable the children to take the writing tool to the stimulus or the comfortable chair, treating it much more like the back of an envelope than a writing desk. They also allow children to use the word processor in a more flexible way, rather than 'waiting their turn' for the class machine. The children learn that they can plan their time in order to take advantage of the portables, from taking notes and developing written ideas to the final layout and printing of the work. Children in the Wiltshire Laptop Project wrote,

> You can use a laptop anywhere and anytime, unlike a computer that you can't carry around. A laptop is quick and as soon as you press the keys the writing comes up so you can get your work done more quickly than using paper and pencil.
>
> (Lottie Platel, Yr 3, in Eyre, 1993, p. 18)

In 1993, the DfE funded a pilot project in 118 schools having sets of portable computers in order to evaluate the effect of the machines on children's learning. In terms of their writing, children were observed to use portables effectively in the development of the review, revision and refinement of their work and practising styles of writing in given formats. The flexibility of access to the machines seemed to enable them to focus on the whole set of skills needed in the writing process. The children's awareness of the ease with which they could return to and correct spellings, punctuation, ideas and structure provided insight into the 'hierarchy of concerns' of the writing process. (Stradling *et al.*, 1994).

Another opportunity to explore the effects of technology on writing is provided by electronic communications. The immediacy of connections made by fax and electronic mail (e-mail) not only enables messages to be sent quickly, but can also affect the context and style of that writing. Regular users of e-mail comment that they adopt a more informal style in their on-line communications, a mode between writing and conversation, letter and telephone. The writer can also adopt different roles, concealing from the recipient such features as age, gender and any difficulties in speed and accuracy of writing, creating a conversation without the usual assumptions about characteristics which can constrain and limit interaction. Electronic mail also provides the opportunity to widen the audience for one's writing, from an electronic pen-pal to a world-wide interest group.

The National Council for Educational Technology (NCET) funded a variety of uses for electronic mail in schools in the Communications Collaborative Project (NCET, 1991b). Schools in Hampshire and Oxfordshire, for example, shared and developed pupils' poetry. The activity had authenticity, in that the exchanges were between writers and a genuine audience, and the children took on the role of constructive critics themselves, not relying on the teacher as arbiter. Other projects included pen-pal exchanges between schools in cities, rural areas and different countries; participation in live adventure games; an electronic 'writer in residence', working with children in several schools to develop a narrative; children collecting data in residential field centres and linking with those back at school, who could use it in their ongoing work; and schools in different parts of the country working together on a topic to study and compare dialects.

Just as the traditional ideas of the nature of correspondence are extended by electronic communications, so the experience of writers and readers can also be altered in the use of IT to create 'hypertext'. Marshall McLuhan commented that 'Gutenberg made everyone a reader. Xerox made everyone a publisher' – and now personal computers are making everyone an author (Woolley, 1993). Ideas of hypertext, or interactive, non-linear reading or narratives, are not confined to the world of computing. Tristan Tsara, the Dada-ist author, constructed poems by drawing words from a hat, and the novelist William Burroughs developed a 'cut-up' method of writing, urging the reader to divide the written page into four pieces and rearrange them to destroy the control of the narrative. In 1945 Vannevar Bush described a 'Memex' machine which would create links and 'trails' between items of information. The computer is an ideal machine for such a task, storing vast numbers of 'items', from digits to documents, displaying them for the reader and providing the means and opportunity to create connections between those items. These connections can be set up by the author to guide the reader along certain routes in the text, but they can also provide a number of choices which the reader can make in order to produce a less predictable journey through the narrative.

Early examples of the reader's control of movement were the adventure games of the 1970s and 1980s, where 'the imaginary worlds lodged in the writer's head turned into virtual worlds lodged in the computer's memory' (Woolley, 1993, p. 155). Players of the game could create the story by making decisions about the routes through these 'worlds' often predictably populated by a cast of thousands of elves. More recent advances in power, memory and communication in new technology have enabled the distinction between authors and readers to become blurred. A reader can not only call up a text and annotate or alter it, but also search through that text, explore connections and cross-references, access related information from networks of databases around the world, and incorporate these new elements into the 'original' – electronic browsing, cutting and pasting.

The technology to make these types of connection is now available in schools. In the 1980s, children in a London primary school participated in a 'Worlds' project in which they developed simple versions of interactive narratives. Some designed adventure games set in castles, space ships and haunted houses, allowing access to rooms in a number of ways, whilst others designed a series of linked Teletext pages which the reader could choose to find out more about the class visit to a pond. The children noticed the similarities between the two activities: 'Moving through my pages is just like putting the rooms together, isn't it Miss?' Although the IT resources used in this project are now exhibited in an Archive of Educational Technology, the general principle was clear: authors providing readers with opportunities to make decisions and interact with the 'text'.

'Authoring packages' such as HyperCard, HyperStudio, Guide, Genesis and Magpie, can be used by children to incorporate text, sound and visual images and link the items for presentation and exploration. Although at present attention is given to the compilation of the 'multimedia pages', the development of this way of working has great potential for children and teachers to think about the nature of the connections they make, the choices they provide and the opportunities they give the readers to extend the work and make it their own.

RESERVATIONS

The previous discussion has been in rosy terms of using IT to support some of the elements of the writing process, providing opportunities to develop IT capability and insights into the writing process itself for the children. Some have argued that IT is, at last, the tool to enable children to become real writers in control of the writing process.

The actual picture in many classrooms may not be so rosy. Interesting issues are raised by the use of IT in writing, from the concerns of authors that it can stultify the creative process to the concerns of teachers that the level of use of IT is very low, and that collaboration can be a grand term for children taking all day to type in alternate lines of a previously written story.

In a conversation with a friend who is a novelist, poet and translator, using a word processor daily, he remarked that the powerful facility to modify and move text can become a barrier to the rigours of composition, giving a false sense of ease in a difficult creative process. Daniel Chandler states that 'word processing is the celebration of form versus meaning', giving work a tidy and finished appearance which it may not warrant, or as a child observed, 'The computer makes my writing look better than it is' (Chandler, 1990, p. 170). The screen provides a very narrow window on to the text which limits a sense of the overall structure, despite the use of outliners and planners. Daniel Chandler quotes the journalist Nancy Banks-Martin saying, 'It's difficult to get a shape unless you see it in front of you. There isn't room on the screen for a beginning, middle and an end'. (Chandler, 1990, p. 170). Some writers prefer to start composing with a sharp HB pencil and narrow-lined paper, some leave scraps and scribbles around the house while ideas are incubated and hatched.

All these folk, however, are mature writers, who have an understanding of the development of the whole process from composition to publication and are able to choose a suitable tool – pens, word processors, hypertext packages or sticky telephone message pads. Children as developing writers need to gain insight into the demands of the writing process and have a range of experiences in order to make choices from media available appropriate to their style and mood.

Some researchers in the field of artificial intelligence have investigated the possibilities of using IT to provide guidance and insight into writing. Sharples (1988) used a series of programs to help children 'construct' their writing from component words and phrases according to developing rules of grammar and syntax, viewing language as an 'object to be shaped and revised' (p. 135). Yazdani (1989) has also demonstrated the 'improvement' of writing by allocating the task to the machine, which followed rules about story writing to generate texts. Other writers such as John Beynon (1993c), however, are critical of this approach, as it 'technologizes' the writing process, ignoring the role of social interaction, collaboration and the way in which children learn through writing as they do through talking and reading. The computer is being asked to take over the processes which are needed to develop literacy and competence in communication.

The importance of the nature and quality of interaction of children, teachers and computers in the context of learning to write is reiterated by Graham Peacock (1993). He noted that attention to spelling and the appearance of the final product did increase when children used a word processor, but that the higher-level discussion of the meaning and structure of the writing did not necessarily occur spontaneously around the keyboard, needing to be drawn out by careful encouragement and questioning from the teacher. This is supported by Ronald Owston, who focused on how computers affected the way a particular teacher taught writing and the ways in which the children worked. 'Teachers need guidance and assistance in understanding and interpreting how computers affect what they do in the classroom' (Owston, 1993, p. 240).

WRITING AND IT IN THE CLASSROOM

What can teachers do, given that a child spending time in the presence of a word processor does not automatically develop into a mature writer? In planning experiences for the children it is essential to understand the underlying principle of the task and set up the activity to focus on it appropriately for the children. Never stop asking the question, 'What's the *point* of doing this?'

To encourage composition and structuring, involve the children in preparation, discussion, brainstorming and making notes in many different ways, from drawing spider diagrams to word lists. Creating a concept keyboard overlay which provides key words and phrases would enable the children to make a start with their ideas without having to type everything out in the early stages. Let the children print out their work many times along the way and lay it out in front of them in order to represent, check and amend the structure if necessary.

Focus on editing and manipulation techniques by providing starting points or frameworks, such as beginnings, endings and jumbles of stories. These will need an operational knowledge of the writing package in order to move around the document, delete, insert, copy and paste, use a spell checker and thesaurus, as well as providing the opportunity for discussion and debate about spellings, sentences and order. Use the word processor yourself to comment on and edit a piece of writing, inserting your suggestions clearly in the children's work by using a different font or style of printing. Let the children create picture poems by changing the style and format of letters, sentences and paragraphs.

Organize the tasks to take place over time, allowing the children time to save, print and retrieve their work. This will reinforce the need to reflect upon their writing, giving the children the opportunity to think and talk with their peers and with the teacher. Encourage the children to keep and annotate their early drafts to show how their ideas have developed.

Think carefully about an approach to collaboration and group work in the classroom. This is a vital concern in providing a learning environment characterized by high-quality interaction, thinking and activity. It involves far more than 'seating arrangements'; the organization of access to IT resources reflects the teacher's views about purposeful ways of working for groups and individuals.

Involve the children in the consideration of the destination and audience for their writing. They need to think about whether their work is for a personal notebook, presentation in a wall display, part of a poster or an item in a newsletter or magazine. They also need to think about the style of their writing, from factual reporting to writing in a genre. The nature and number of people reading their work will determine the type of IT resource used – a word processor, a desktop publisher, electronic mail or an authoring package.

Discuss the advantages and disadvantages of producing their writing with IT and compare it with other methods. Does IT offer opportunities to write in new ways? When would other methods be more appropriate? When is it best to use a combination of methods? Is enjoyment and novelty enough? Does it help them to develop a critical and confident approach to their work which allows mistakes to be seen and learned from?

After observing children and teachers working with IT to develop their writing, Peacock concluded that,

> if there is an uncritical response to the word processor and an assumption that it will by itself usher in a golden age of writing then we will be missing an opportunity to examine the way that children write.
>
> (Peacock, 1993, p. 97).

VISUAL ART AND IT

Although the themes of composition, manipulation, refining and presentation also apply to processes in the visual arts, there are significant differences between the nature of text and the nature of a visual image. The most notable is perhaps the physical link between the marks on the page and the person who writes or draws those marks. The printing press has long removed the ideas and content of the written word from the handwritten signature of the author. We can still be fascinated by the original manuscripts of Jane Austen, George Eliot, Bach and Beethoven in the British Museum, but most text reaches us in printed form.

Visual arts are a direct expression of ideas and techniques, a direct link to the artists and their distinctive, physical 'finger-print'. The movement of the pen, brush, knife or rag is part of the creative work itself, giving texture, interacting with other media such as the paper, canvas or clay and reflecting the artist's individual 'signature'. There have been considerable advances in the potential of IT to represent these physical expressions, in both the handling and presentation of infor-mation. Computers are becoming more powerful in speed and memory and so can handle more complex visual informa-tion provided by a variety of methods, from drawings to photographs, and present the finished product on screens, printers, plotters and film. It is the tension between the new possibilities for creativity that IT can bring and the constraints that current technology imposes that makes this an exciting and interesting area in visual arts education.

Kevin Mathieson (1993) summarized children's visual education as comprising three main elements:

1 perception through observation, memory and imagination, visualizing ideas and drawing upon a wide range of resources from the environment;

2 the use of materials as media, developing the ability to select and control materials, tools and techniques to express ideas in a visual language, using colour, line, shape and pattern in two and three dimensions;

3 knowledge and understanding of the language of art as expressed by themselves and by others.

Art education also implies an encouragement of creativity. Free expression with a range of materials can be original, but not necessarily creative. Woods and Barrow argued that there needs to be a recognition of quality and excellence, and that this is supported by three requirements:

1 We have to avoid instilling in children the idea that everything is known and determined, and that they must subserve the acknowledged experts in any field and cannot follow their own distinctive way of looking at things.

2 We have to promote ingenuity and imagination so that individuals are capable of making the imaginative leaps necessary for breaking new ground in any sphere.

3 We have to produce skill and understanding in any given sphere, for without these how, except by chance, is the individual going to be a good scientist, artist or whatever; how is he going to have the excellence that is part of creativity?

(Woods and Barrow, 1988, p. 14)

Children need a wealth of experiences in a variety of contexts to be able to draw together these elements of perception, media, knowledge, understanding and creativity. IT provides a medium which can be compared with other media, such as paint or photography, but it also offers unique features which give opportunities for new techniques and expression.

IT AND GRAPHICS: WHAT ARE COMPUTERS GOOD AT?

What are the facilities that have encouraged widespread use of IT by graphic artists and designers and increasing exploitation by fine artists? Computers have to be powerful in speed and memory to process, store, display and make accessible a complex visual image incorporating line, points, shape and colour. They process and represent digital information in a world which is visually analogue, or continuous. Designers of graphic packages therefore use the computer's power either, as described by Scrimshaw (1988), to mimic the traditional techniques of an artist – freehand sketching, colouring with paint, spraying, smudging, and using pens and brushes of different shapes and sizes – or to enhance the processing facilities to represent mathematical relationships to draw accurate shapes, curves and linked lines.

CREATING IMAGES

Most IT packages present a model of an artist working with a blank piece of paper on the screen and choosing particular tools, palettes and motifs for different effects. There are various ways to communicate with the graphics package to produce a working image:

- A mouse is the familiar tool with many computers, pointing, clicking and dragging over the screen, selecting and using the required tools.

- A pen and 'digitizing tablet' (an electronic drawing pad) can be used to simulate the drawing action of the artist, responding to the speed and pressure that the artist uses with the pen with much more sensitivity than a mouse. This allows more familiar and finer movements of the pen or brush.

- 'Scanning' or digitizing images is a very useful and

powerful technique which can overcome some of the problems of 'mouse control'. Images produced in other media, such as photographs, drawings and collages, can be captured by the scanner or camera and converted into a digital form that the computer can read and store. These digitized images can then be manipulated and worked with on the screen using the tools available in the graphics package.

- 'Clip art' is a set of images produced by other artists provided on a disc or CD ROM for other users to select, copy and paste into their own work for illustration or development.

PAINTING AND DRAWING

'Painting' and 'drawing' are actually two very different processes on the computer. Some of the graphics packages will only do one of these types of activity, whilst some will integrate the two. It is important to understand the difference between the two in IT terms, as they can be used for very different purposes and effects.

'Painting' allows the artist to produce an image rather as you would produce a picture painted onto a piece of paper. Marks, colours and shapes are fixed onto the paper, often overlapping and combining with each other to build up a whole image. Sections of that image can be cut out, transformed or distorted in some way and moved about the canvas, but the lines, colours and shapes cannot be separated from each other once they have been put down on the canvas. The picture elements or 'pixels' are actually very small blocks of colour represented on the screen, just as fragments of a mosaic combine to give an overall visual effect. It is possible to 'zoom' in on areas of these pixels and enlarge them in order to manipulate them more finely.

'Drawing' on the computer has a different purpose and a different approach. Visual objects including text, can be drawn onto the paper in a variety of shapes, sizes, colours and patterns. The computer processes these 'objects' as mathematical relationships between the points, thus being able to represent sophisticated shapes, curves and lines very accurately. These objects are treated separately by the computer and can therefore be moved and manipulated relative to the position of other objects. A yellow ellipse with a red border and a blue irregular pentagon could be drawn, moved on top of each other, moved behind each other, joined together so that they moved together as a group, or made transparent so that one could be viewed through the other. Elements of the visual image can be produced and placed with great accuracy, rather like separate pieces of acetate being moved over and under each other to produce particular collage effects. The elements of the image are therefore not fixed on the canvas as in 'painting', but can be moved, manipulated and assembled.

THE MIMICRY OF ARTISTS' TOOLS

Line, colour and pattern can be investigated using tools such as a brush, a pen, a spray can, a roller brush, and a palette which can contain colours and patterns to be dipped into. In a graphics package, these tools are often represented by familiar icons chosen to indicate the type of tool – such as a brush or spray can! The 'fill' tool, which can flood areas with colour or pattern, can be represented as a paint roller, jug or paint pot to associate it with the image of paint spilling or covering large areas. The size and shape of these tools can be altered, and the range of colours and patterns available in the palette will depend upon the sophistication of the package and IT system being used. The tools are usually selected and manipulated by pointing, clicking and dragging with the mouse.

It is often useful to introduce a new graphics package for exploration by limiting the number of tools to be used. It is interesting to see how the children can develop work on size and pattern using only a few colours and varying the size and shape of the brush. Some packages enable the user or teacher to make visible a limited menu of tools to avoid the 'paper' becoming cluttered.

Children in a reception class, using a package called Revelation on Acorn computers to paint pictures of boats, were able to choose whether to use a brush or a pen to make the marks for the outlines of the boat, mast and sails, and to select a colour from the palette of 256 colours. They experimented with the different effects caused by moving the brush slowly or quickly and the possibilities of rubbing out unwanted marks by picking up the background colour with a 'dropper' and painting over the problem with a thick brush. They used the spray can to mix blues, greens and white for the sea and spray, and the 'paint pot' to flood areas of the boat, sea and sky. They were clear about the effects they wanted to create and asked each other and their assistant for tips. They were very much in control of the tools and were confident in using IT. A boy in another reception class was chatting about the ways he used the computer to paint pictures: 'You know, it's quite clever because it will go over colours'; but he later commented on a disappointing print out from a faulty printer: 'This computer annoys people when they want black and it goes green. It can make them *very* annoyed.'

ENHANCING THE TRADITIONAL TOOLS: MANIPULATION, TRANSFORMATION AND SUBSTITUTION

The production of geometric shapes and curves on the screen which can be manipulated in their own right has been mentioned above. These tools enable the children to draw accurately without needing fine control of the mouse, which is a rather clumsy implement. But whether it is by painting and drawing with the tools, importing some clip art or scanning an image from other media, the production of the image on the screen is actually the first stage of the process. The power of using IT in art is in the range of manipulations of visual images that is available. Areas of the painted image, or objects which have been drawn, can be selected and then deleted, moved and copied, just like text in a word processor. There is also the opportunity to transform these selected areas by changing colours, distorting shapes, shearing, flipping, rotating, scaling up and down, and repeating the image to create a range of effects. Adjustments and experiments can be tried, considered and rejected, the results being erased, or printed and saved in a series of images to show the process and progress of the work.

Children in a reception class also working on the topic of

'water' had looked at a postcard of Monet's *Water Lilies*. They chose an area of the water that they liked and tried to reproduce the effect on the computer using a small brush, spray and related colours. They then selected this 'effect' and made it into a motif, which then became the pattern or paint used by the brush instead of a colour. These lovely detailed patterns were then used in broad brush strokes in a new design contributing to a class collage on water. Older children in a year 6 class using the same package were able to develop the idea of using a motif in their work. They used curves, regular shapes and pen marks to design a footprint by observing the soles of their shoes. This footprint was produced in the centre of the screen. It was then carefully selected, 'cut out' and made into a motif, which was transformed in a variety of ways, from repeated rotations to a range of distortions taking the image far away from the original.

Choosing and using the appropriate tool for the task lies at the heart of both art education and the development of IT capability. IT provides opportunities for active experimentation, immediate feedback, reworking, substitution, and transformations which would be difficult and time consuming for young children to implement using other media. Much of this type of work would have taken many hours in a dark room or by a photocopier to produce working copies for experimentation and fragmentation. The ability to save, retrieve and rework a piece, showing the progression of ideas and techniques, is also important, as is the variety of ways of capturing images and getting a variety of outputs for the finished product, from a coloured print out to textiles and video.

LIMITATIONS

An obvious limitation of the medium is the lack of physical response as the artist tries to produce marks and effects with tools which are crude when compared to the ways in which the human touch can influence pencil, charcoal, paint, clay, metal and fibres. Peter Scrimshaw (1988) discussed the importance of dexterity and delicacy of touch in the craft skills in order to develop a visual appreciation of works of art. Although there are advantages to some children in being able to produce visual effects without having to worry about their developing motor skills and hand–eye co-ordination, many teachers of art would wish to develop this kinaesthetic element in visual education. There is inherent pleasure and purpose in learning to work physically with different and difficult media. The fine gradations in texture brought about by the control of pressure cannot yet be reproduced with current technology in schools, although there are advances in more sophisticated systems.

There can also be a tendency to conformity to the effects which can be easily produced, such as shapes, points and lines, rather than experimenting with other possibilities. Some artists have complained that the images have no distinctive 'fingerprint', the accuracy of the drawing detracting from the distinctive nature of the artist's touch. There has also been discussion of the emotional response to new technology, some viewing it as high-status, modern and prestigious, others lamenting the lack of individuality in its effects and mechanistic image. It has been noted, though, that many of these comments are similar to the cries against the new technology of photography when it first appeared.

ART AND IT IN THE CLASSROOM

What challenges and experiences can we give to children to develop their awareness of IT as a medium in visual education? As in supporting children's writing, it is important to consider the underlying purpose of the activity, to provide opportunities for IT capability as well as learning in the curriculum. It is therefore interesting to use computer tools alongside traditional tools to highlight the advantages and limitations of each. Mathieson (1993) describes a number of lively ideas to give the children insight into the nature of the task and the characteristics of the tools and materials chosen. These experiences contrast and combine traditional media and computer art, whether by using each other as starting points and planning tools, or by incorporating the different media in a final product.

Mark making and lines can be explored by using traditional pencils, charcoals and crayons and comparing the effects with

47

specific computer tools, such as a brush or spray can. The swirls and curls of lines produced with a mouse can be developed further with other materials, such as string prints, rubbings or wire. The remarkable effects of colour mixing and juxtaposition can be emphasized by comparing the qualities of colour produced by paints and inks with that of colour produced by 'light' on the screen. The choices offered by different palettes and the opportunities to adjust or substitute screen colours allow more immediate experimentation than some traditional media.

After working with a variety of materials for print making, from vegetable sections to clay blocks, it is interesting to explore the possibilities of computer printing. Elements of the screen image can be copied, rotated and transformed, and a series of reproductions can be developed. The selection of motifs for printing can be extended to cutting up, rearrangement and pasting, forming collages of patterns. Such effects seen on the screen can also be used as starting points for further interpretation and development: print outs can be incorporated into collages of textured and 3D materials, the lines of the printer followed in weaving, and blocks of a 'zoomed' image echoed in embroidery.

The process of trying out an idea and developing techniques to express it can be monitored and discussed by taking print outs of the work in progress or saving successive stages. The facility for saving, letting time elapse for reflection and returning to retrieve and experiment with the image is a powerful aspect of IT. Discarded ideas or physical mistakes can be undone or incorporated into new ideas, not to save paint or paper but because being able to do so opens up new possibilities.

SO WHAT'S NEW?

In addition to providing a new medium of computer graphics and digitized images, IT can make a unique contribution to art education, creating experiences for the children which would not have been available without new technology.

The ability to capture and digitize an image – that is, convert it to a form which the computer can store and manipulate – creates an immediacy and a degree of control for the children. This can be compared with the time and physical involvement required with other media, and discussed in terms of advantages and limitations. Images can be stored, worked with, developed and saved to show the progression of ideas over time. Manipulation, transformation and animation can be explored, connections between images established, and pictures incorporated with sound and text to develop multimedia presentation. The computer can present children with experiences usually only possible in a production studio.

The advent of CD ROMS into primary classrooms has literally opened doors to the galleries of the world. Reproductions of pictures from, for example, the National Gallery in London, with associated information and interactive guides, are available to children and teachers, whether researching portraiture or Poussin. There are a great number of visual images available on CD ROM, and although the tactile quality of turning the pages of a beautifully illustrated book cannot be matched on the screen, the potential for interaction, following and setting up connections between images and ideas is exciting.

An example of this potential is illustrated in 'From Silver to Silicon', a project involving a group of twenty photographers, media galleries and commercial production companies. The photographers were encouraged to use new technologies to create 'electronic essays' of photographs. They were able to guide and interact with the viewer through the 'passages' of a 'virtual gallery' existing in the computer's memory. The visitors to the gallery could look at images, animations, manipulations and distortions, the presentation being always 'in progress', being developed in response to contributors' suggestions (Evans, 1994).

The area of fractal geometry (complex expressions of mathematical relationships, developed by Benoit Mandelbrot) has led to the generation of extraordinary and unpredictable visual images, resembling the chaotic and asymmetrical forms of nature. Art as an expression of mathematics is not new – Islamic tile patterns and Gabo's sculptures represent such visual expressions – but the computer's speed in processing mathematical functions and power in depicting them visually make new techniques available to us. These techniques for modelling relationships in two and three dimensions have produced startling images of landscapes, coastlines, skies and combinations which can represent new worlds. Mike Cooley, president of the International Research Institute in Human Centred Systems, commented that in the fifteenth century, the Duke of Urbino surrounded himself in his study with pictures and images to provoke thought and imagination. What marvellous possibilities lie in the power of IT to develop new images to stimulate the mind.

IT has a distinctive contribution to make in the communication of information, whether it be in text, visual images or sound. The processes of composition and structure, manipulation and transformation, drafting, editing and presentation are supported by the use of IT, from the first marks on the page to the final showing to an audience. Such tools can also provide insight into the nature of the communication itself and the decisions that have to be made by writers and artists in order to express themselves.

The opportunities and constraints that IT tools present allow teachers and children to think about the purpose of the task, the skills required and the appropriate techniques available. IT can also be considered as a new agent for communication, reaching wide and disparate audiences, integrating media and representing new imagery. Picasso gave a 'Statement' in 1923 (see Picasso, 1923) in which he said, 'Art does not evolve by itself, the ideas of people change and with them their mode of expression' (p. 264). It remains to be seen whether IT is just another medium, or a catalyst for such a new mode of expression.

CHAPTER 3
Handling Information

What is information handling?

The ability to handle and know what to do with information does not require 'information technology'. Equally, skill with IT resources does not necessarily reflect an understanding of effective information handling. That includes activities ranging from checking a railway timetable to comparing standards of living in different parts of the country by interpreting data from the national census, and can be described as the progression through the processes of collecting, organizing, storing, retrieving, manipulating, checking, analysing, interpreting and presenting information. We deal with these processes in order to answer questions, solve problems, gain evidence, test hypotheses and build up our knowledge. Underlying the physical activities of information handling are the questions which need to be asked in order to guide the seeker and presenter of information to a satisfactory conclusion, the most important ones being, 'Why are we going to gather information?' 'What is it that we want to know?' and 'What is the point of the enquiry?'

Identifying the purpose and direction of an enquiry is the first step. A range of skills can be used to collect information: asking relevant questions, listening, observing, recording and making notes, reading to skim material and reading in detail, using directories and reference material. There is also a need for skills in organizing and classifying information to assist in systematic retrieval – as some of us will know to our cost after frantic rustling through papers in piles marked 'Miscellaneous' and 'Other'.

A framework of nine questions was devised by Michael Marland (1981) to guide the progress of the work of handling information, whether that be a scientific investigation, developing a topic or writing an assignment:

1 What do I need to know?
2 Where could I go?
3 How do I get to the information?
4 Which resources shall I use?
5 How shall I use the resources?
6 What should I make a record of?
7 Have I got the information I need?
8 How should I present it?
9 What have I achieved?

This framework was developed further, identifying the questions, skills and abilities required and the concepts underlying the activities, in order to relate it closely to the National Curriculum. This emphasizes the need for information skills across the curriculum and underlies the ways in which primary children can acquire them through their ongoing work, rather than being taught a series of disembedded techniques (NCET, 1990).

Freeman and Levett (1986) identified a 'common core' of skills in designing, interrogating and evaluating a body of data, but highlighted the subject-specific nature of the approach to data collection and analysis. An historian and a scientist would approach their sources of information and methods of interpretation in different ways; the skills and expertise needed in locating and transcribing a primary source document would be different from those of setting up an experiment to log and record data for statistical analysis.

The 'common core' of skills can be elaborated by looking more closely at the stages of design, interrogation and evaluation, the tasks required in each of those stages, and the combination of skills needed to support these tasks (Southall, 1992). These stages, tasks and skills are just as applicable to cards kept in a shoe box, questionnaires stored in a drawer or lists pinned to the wall as they are to a computer file:

Stage One ... Design

Tasks required:
Establish the purpose of the task
Decide what information is needed and where it will be found

Select appropriate resources to carry out the task

Appraise likely sources of information and identify the most appropriate

Collect the information in an appropriate way, e.g. research, observation, experiment, counting, measuring and recording

Refine the information in a suitable format e.g. level of accuracy, use of codes

Organise the information into an appropriate form

Skills required:

Planning, interpreting, analysing, hypothesising, predicting, formulating, designing, collecting, measuring, organising

Stage Two ... Interrogation

Tasks required:

Make hypotheses and formulate questions to test them ... selecting, searching, sorting, calculating, counting

Select and retrieve the resulting information

Record the results

Skills required:

Investigating, analysing, reasoning, logic, formulating, recording

Stage Three ... Evaluation

Tasks required:

Process the information; interpret and make inferences appropriate to the purpose of the task

Explain the results; draw conclusions and make further hypotheses

Extrapolate and make generalisations about findings

Present the findings in an appropriate way e.g. text, graphics, pictures etc

Communicate findings, interpretation and conclusions

Evaluate the task; make further hypotheses for testing; quantify work done; consider the relevance of the task; how it was carried out and how it relates to others

Skills required:

Interpreting, analysing, synthesising, inferring, generalising, presenting, communicating, evaluating.

(Southall, 1992, p. 14)

In an 'information society', these questions, techniques and skills are crucial to those who wish to have some control over their access to and use of information. Michael Marland expressed this as follows:

the powerful person is the one who can formulate the question that is at the heart of the problem; search for sources of ideas, argument and information; select and reject these; organise the results; and present a report.

(Marland, 1991)

In our primary classrooms, we wish to develop an understanding of the range of skills needed in order to deal with information meaningfully.

What do children learn through information handling?

Developing a spirit of enquiry lies at the heart of learning, making connections and building knowledge. It is a central challenge for all teachers. The information skills discussed do not just 'appear', but have to be taught, developed and encouraged through the context of the children's learning across the curriculum. Alistair Ross, a teacher whose children used information handling in various and exciting ways, stated:

My broad aims in teaching are to encourage children to conjecture about their world and their society, to test and to communicate their findings and thus to have a degree of control over their environment. Various skills are needed to accomplish these aims, but I believe that such skills are best acquired in the achievement of these aims, not as isolated exercises ... The necessary skills may change as society and technology change.

(Ross, 1984b, p. 64)

When children are handling information they do not just learn about the results of enquiry, or the information skills required; they also learn about the processes of learning itself and what is needed in an approach to problem solving and study. Information handling can be seen as an interactive process (Ross, 1984a), which enables the children to develop more autonomy in their learning as participators and creators, not just spectators (Southall, 1992).

Through information handling, children can learn to:

- use the real world of their direct experience for the observation, collection and recording of data;

- discuss, analyse and generalize from their experiences in order to make connections between themselves and the wider world, and extend that experience to include other sources of information;

- pose good questions in an enquiry, that is, questions which have relevance and purpose in their experience;

- think about observations in order to explain them; analysing and categorizing objects, events and ideas; noting similarities and differences;

- make and test hypotheses;

- use formal reasoning and logic to plan investigations;

- describe their observations;

- think about the significance of their findings;

- display and communicate them in an appropriate way, through narrative, statistics or graphical images.

In displaying and communicating their findings, children have the opportunity to understand and use statistics, based on their experiences of working with information. Alderson defines statistics as 'the area of study that deals with the collection, description and presentation of numerical data and the drawing of conclusions from them' (Alderson, 1992, p. 111). However, the principles of his discussion can be extended to broader issues of children learning to deal with information. He reminds us that children 'will all be "consumers" of other people's data, especially through the media. Those who have developed a critical eye will be able to make informed decisions about what is presented.' (1992, p. 120).

What does IT contribute to the 'spirit of enquiry'?

It is in this area that IT demonstrates its contribution as a tool, a resource for learning and a catalyst in thinking. As a tool it takes on the donkey work of processing and displaying information. As a resource for learning it provides insight into the nature of the subjects being studied – whether history, science, mathematics or geography – each requiring, at some stage, distinctive methods of data collection and interpretation, as described by Freeman and Levett (1986). As a catalyst in thought, it organizes and presents information to the learner and provides the opportunity to develop higher-order skills of analysis, interpretation and evaluation (Ross, 1984b; Southall, 1992).

IT has the capacity to store large amounts of data which can be searched quickly and updated flexibly and easily, just as in communicating in text, pictures and sound. It may well be quicker to flick through an address book to find all the Simkins family under 'S' than to switch on the computer and interrogate a database, but if all the residents in postcode area BN2 were needed for a neighbourhood campaign meeting, the computer could retrieve that information much more quickly and flexibly. As well as being able to store and retrieve information in the twinkling of an eye, a computer can process the data to perform mathematical and statistical operations and display the results in a variety of required forms – alphabetical lists, labelled pictures and graphs displayed as bar, line or pie charts, in 3D if required. A bar graph of modes of travelling to school, a pie chart of the proportions of children having school meals, or a scattergraph of the relationship between height and foot size can be more powerful ways to represent and 'tell the story' about the data than a list or a narrative.

Jean Underwood has described the advantages of using IT in data handling in that it allows rapid and increasingly complex manipulations of data; it offers the opportunity for children to collate and interrogate their own material from the environment; and it reduces the amount of work required that is not actually part of the learning process, such as looking at relationships rather than just counting (Underwood, 1994). She has also emphasized in many areas of her work how thinking skills are actively encouraged by using data storage and retrieval systems for questioning, hypothesis testing and classification (Underwood and Underwood, 1990). She argues that there are positive educational reasons for using IT in information handling, in that it:

- stimulates classificatory ability
- facilitates multiple representations of data
- facilitates the comparison of data
- facilitates the manipulation of large data sets
- encourages the skills of selection of data and modes of representing that data
- encourages the development of questioning skills
- encourages an understanding of the scientific method and the development of hypothesis-testing skills

(Underwood, 1994, p. 86)

As discussed at the beginning of this chapter, we want children to develop not only skills in research and information retrieval, but also an understanding of how information is collected and organized and what kinds of decision have to be made about presentation and use. Children are therefore given the opportunity to observe, sort, classify and count – vegetables, traffic, favourite TV programmes or packets of crisps. Primary classrooms can be cluttered with clip boards, survey forms, record charts and bar graphs, showing that much activity is going on in the first few stages of information handling. These processes provide insight into the structure and presentation of information, but can reach a point where the analysis and interpretation of the information is crowded out by the busyness of collection and display. IT can be used to support the whole process and can help children move from collection to analysis.

How can different models of information handling support classroom work?

The way that information is organized and structured will affect the ways in which it can be accessed and interrogated. It is therefore very important that the organization is related to the original question and purpose of the enquiry. Different types of data-handling software will present different frameworks for the organization of the data file, from simple decision trees requiring a 'yes/no' answer to complex networks of databases all over the world accessed by key words. The most common types of database resource used in primary classrooms are:

- binary or branching tree structures;
- free text databases using key words;
- flat-file databases, from which information is retrieved by a set form of questions;
- hierarchical databases, in which information is linked by prescribed connections;
- relational databases, which can be accessed through a query language, but provide a large and flexible set of connections between items in the database.

The application of these different types of database structure is outlined below, and it is important that teachers and children understand which is the most appropriate type for the problem in hand.

BINARY OR BRANCHING TREE DATABASES

The 'binary tree' programs, such as Branch, Sorting Game, Animal and IDelta, enable the children to sort objects or events by asking questions to which the answer is a clear 'yes' or 'no'. This clear answer will lead down a 'branch' to the next question, the answer to which will lead down another branch until there are no more choices and a clear definition, description or name is given. Setting up such a database requires careful thought in devising questions. They must be clear enough to enable the user to give a definite answer, whether by using previous knowledge, observing items or events very closely, or going off to do more research. Observation, categorization and classification need to be employed by the person setting up the file, in order to devise effective questions which in turn encourage the user to develop such skills in order to answer them.

Setting up a binary tree database brings challenges not only in mathematics, with sorting and classifying, but also in language, in expressing questions clearly enough to make powerful distinctions. A reception class that I was visiting had done lots of work on boats during the previous few weeks. They were using the Branch program with their teacher's help to set up a datafile of their boats, to help visitors to the class see what they knew about these. They selected ten examples, from trawlers to dredgers and lifeboats, and started to ask questions to distinguish each from the rest. 'Has it got an engine?' 'Does it have sails?' and 'Does it rescue people?' were all suggested. Several children realized that all the boats could rescue people if necessary and that a more particular question would be needed. This activity relied on the children making connections between the knowledge they had built up about boats in their topic work and expressing them clearly in order to explain to someone else the differences and similarities.

Classifying objects by close observation and discussion can also be supported by working with binary trees. Describing and identifying items such as leaves, pictures of aircraft, sets of bottles or transport toys will draw the children's attention to the variety of ways of sorting and classifying and the arbitrary nature of some of the criteria which could be used. A group of year 5 children working with winter twigs realized that they could make their binary trees (no pun intended) appear more balanced and elegant if they could define a first question which would divide the pile into two even groups, rather than focus on the immediate characteristics of one item. For example, 'Does it have leaves?' would divide the deciduous and evergreen twigs clearly, but 'Has it got knobbly bark?' was not as clear cut. The questions and language used by the children and the criteria set for decision-making are differentiated according to the children's needs and abilities, the structure of the program being very open-ended and versatile, enabling the children to focus on observation and expression.

FREE TEXT DATABASES

These databases enable the children to enter text which describes objects or events in their own words, in narrative or note form. Important 'key words' in that text can be selected and marked. Those key words are then associated directly with that object and can be used at a later date to access the record and description very quickly. A program such as Datasweet contains a key word facility which enables children to set up a number of 'cards', in which information in the form of text and pictures could be entered on dinosaurs, for example. Key words such as the name of the dinosaur and characteristics such as 'herbivore' or 'carnivore' could be highlighted, and used to retrieve subsets of dinosaurs or particular examples at a later date.

FLAT-FILE DATABASES

'Flat-file' databases are used widely, and this framework is the one that many people commonly think of as a 'database'. It is modelled on the metaphor of a card index, rather like a box of cards used for names and addresses. The 'file' is the box, a set of cards with a particular theme such as birds, boats, volcanoes or addresses. Each 'record' is a card associated with a different object or person, and each of those records has a set of 'fields' or headings, such as 'Name', 'Address', 'Telephone number'. Sorting and searching through the database is similar to 'riffling' through the cards, the computer obviously being able to do this electronic riffling more quickly, accurately and flexibly than a human being. The information on these records can also be represented in columns under the fields or headings.

Setting up such a database needs careful thought in designing the 'card' with the right headings or questions and clear indications of the type of answer required. The records can then be searched or sorted by the child using a set form of 'query language'. For example, in searching a database of 'Ourselves' in which some of the physical characteristics of the children had been recorded, a natural question may be 'How many girls have grey eyes?' whereas the query language might have to be expressed as "Eye Colour" contains "grey" and "Sex" = "Female".'

There are many examples of flat-file databases which illustrate the processes the children can go through. Maggie Driscoll, an infant teacher working with a topic of 'Water', asked the children to investigate and record what made the best type of boat for carrying a load across the sand tray. They had to consider the variables of materials, design, size, load carried and what made a 'fair test' in propelling the boats across the pool. (The rather ingenious idea of using the school hoover with its hose fixed backwards to create a breeze raised interesting discussions of health and safety.) In making up record cards for each boat, the children had to think carefully about the headings which would be required and the need for consistent coding of response. The 'cards' for each boat were designed to have eleven fields:

Name	whatever the children decided would describe the boat
Material	what it was made of
Length	at its longest point in cms
Width	at its widest point in cms
Weight	as accurately as we could manage with the scales available
Shape	using the children's descriptions
Mast	whether or not it had one
Sail	whether or not it had one
Distance	how far it travelled along the sand tray in cms
Speed	the time in seconds it took to travel from one end of the tray to the other, timed with a stopwatch
Sinkweight	how much weight we could place on the top of each boat before it sank

(Driscoll, 1987, p. 15)

The results from the cards were then put on to a computer database and various questions asked, such as sorting the data to look at the fastest boat or heaviest load, searching to see which designs were better for speed or load (Driscoll, 1987). It is interesting also in the recording of 'fair test' trials, whether they be of boats, paper darts or packets of crisps, that the children have to recognize the characteristics of different types of data they are dealing with. Names and descriptions are straightforward labels, and numbers such as measurements of distance or price can be dealt with by mathematical rules. Subjective values, however, such as a score out of ten for taste of crisps or aesthetic quality of flight of a dart, are based on personal judgments and need further consideration about their qualities as 'numbers'.

Another interesting example which illustrates the development of lines of enquiry was the census work carried out by children in Fox School in Notting Hill. The children were working with census material from 1871 for the area around their school. Searching through the piles of photocopied census returns, written in the spidery hand of the Victorian enumerator, was a difficult and laborious task which could be done more quickly and efficiently using IT, thus freeing the children to follow through their enquiries.

The children had to think about the ways in which they could design their database using headings drawn from the original census returns and their own research. They used straightforward fields to indicate households, names, sex, marital status and birthplace, but needed to code the occupations in some way to help them to group similar occupations such as washerwoman, laundry woman, laundry assistant. They also needed to devise a field to give map references to show places of birth, from London to the rest of the world.

After entering all the data – 288 records – they started to make their enquiries. Some children searched for a particular address and found out everyone who was living there, from the head of the house to the servants. They wrote diaries to show what life would have been like for this household, using other sources to research areas such as costume, food and the life of servants. Some children investigated the different age populations, finding that the older folk were not born locally, indicating the new building development in Kensington in the mid-nineteenth century. Others found that there was a clear division in the street in that there were many young women between the ages of 15 and 25 in one area, but hardly any in another. The children were not able to explain this disparity and decided to go out to look at the houses in the different areas. The area with a high density of young women was one of large houses which, although in the 1980s they were made into small flats, were once the homes of the wealthy. The area with few young women was one of smaller houses and 'cottages', stylish in the 1980s but homes of artisans in the 1870s. After further research and discussion it was proposed that the young girls had gone into 'service' in the wealthier homes. Further questions could then be asked of the database to see if the young women in service were local, or even from the artisans' cottages down the road!

One enquiry of the database raised a problem which the children's hypotheses could not explain. Observation and further research from a variety of sources were required in order to develop new knowledge about social and economic conditions in the 1870s and changes in those patterns during the twentieth century. Thus the presence of the IT resources for data handling was able to support the children in dealing with large amounts of information, display their findings graphically, and stimulate them to follow through lines of enquiry using higher-order skills of questioning, testing and interpreting.

HIERARCHICAL DATABASES

These are constructed by making links and connections between different elements of information, such as pages of Teletext or cards in a HyperCard stack. A 'web' of connections can be built up so that some 'pages' can be reached from many others, whilst some are only accessible through certain routes. These routes are defined by the person setting up the database. An interesting application of this form of database was developed by some year 4 children who wanted to make their own electronic 'clue book' of birds based on a teletext program called Revolver. Information about types of beak, markings and habitats was researched, entered into the pages in the form of text and chunky graphics, and linked according to the connections the children had designed.

RELATIONAL DATABASES

These databases are set up so that related data is 'marked' and can be accessed very quickly, even though it is not associated with a particular location or record. The links in the network can be explored by the person using the database in a similar way to a flat-file database, but much more flexibly. These databases are becoming more frequent in the primary classroom with the advent of CD ROMs, which can store large amounts of information and 'marked' links. Entire encyclopaedias on CD ROM can be explored by using a form of query language which can access a variety of types of information. A query for 'female' and 'singer' and 'jazz' will find a number of examples, from which I could choose to listen to Billie Holiday whilst looking at her picture.

SPREADSHEETS

A spreadsheet is also a way of organizing data. The framework is one of columns and rows, data being placed in the intersections or 'cells'. This data can include numbers, text and formulae which influence relationships between the data in other cells. The numerical calculations and relationships are displayed in a grid on the screen and can be represented in a variety of forms for interpretation and analysis. For example, in costing a school journey a formula could be constructed to add up all the prices. If a cheap deal on the packed lunches altered the price of the food, then the total charges would change automatically. Although some spreadsheets are designed to be simplified for children's use, the setting up and manipulation of spreadsheet applications is considered to be more appropriate for later KS2 pupils (Cavendish, 1994).

An interesting and simple package for storing and retrieving information, which does not fit easily into these categories, is Touch Explorer, a program which uses the touch on different areas of a concept keyboard to produce text displays of information on the screen. The paper overlay for the concept keyboard is designed – by teachers or children – as pictures or text or both. Touch Explorer is then used to instruct the computer to respond to particular areas of the concept keyboard. For example, a photograph of women harvesting rice in Thailand could be used as an overlay. When different areas of the picture are pressed, information appears on the screen. The complexity and challenge of that information can vary according to the needs and interests of the children, from 'These women are picking rice' to 'What will happen to this rice after it is harvested?' Touch Explorer allows different levels of questions or information to be programmed, and the setting up of files of overlays and questions is a very valuable activity in that it raises issues about the presentation of information – whether to provide straightforward explanations or questions to encourage further research. An intriguing application of Touch Explorer observed in a special school was to give the children a blank overlay which, when pressed, triggered messages on the screen describing parts of a treasure island. The children built up their image of the island on the overlay with drawings and models, responding to the written clues.

Indeed, as Jean Underwood notes (1994), information-handling software in schools is becoming increasingly diverse. The integration of and connection between text and graphics and the technical development in storage capacity and memory of computers mean that children can design and build their own 'shells' to structure information, or use 'off the shelf' frameworks. Data can be compiled for specific topics in the curriculum, such as BodyMapper, a visual database relating to Ourselves, a CD ROM on the Anglo-Saxons, or a prepared spreadsheet with graphics to investigate the contrasts between standards of living in Victorian times and modern times.

Are the demands of information handling changing?

In the early days of using IT in data handling, much emphasis was placed on the importance of the children designing the collection and organization of the data. There is no doubt that the structuring and setting up of a database can help the children to focus on the types of question that they are asking and the ways in which the information can be retrieved. The design of the database required discussion, pilot studies and revision in order to refine the thinking and activity required. Such tasks helped the children in their classificatory abilities and in their understanding of how to approach effective questioning of the database.

With the development of data storage and retrieval discussed previously, people are using more 'off the shelf' data prepared and structured by others, giving access to wide knowledge bases. Associated with this development, therefore, is a shift in the demand for classificatory skills to those of retrieval and selection. Browsing through large amounts of information, however, does not imply an understanding of the connections or a sense of direction in the enqiury, and the time for access to IT resources is too restricted to allow for information retrieval by serendipity. It is therefore important for children to experience these early stages of organizing information in a variety of ways in order to help them build up a 'mental map' of the processes involved in leading to interpretation and presentation.

Developing a mental model of the ways that the computer stores, sorts and searches the data helps children organize and ask the right questions of the information. That is not to say that they need to know technically 'how the computer works', but they should understand the principles of the processes involved. It is therefore helpful if they are given all sorts of 'pre-computer' activities, from straightforward sorting and classifying to complex interrogations:

- Sort objects into sets in different ways.

- Liven up the line to go out to play by playing sorting games – all the people with long hair, all the people with trousers, all the people with long hair *and* trousers, and all the people with long hair *or* trousers.

- Make large picture charts of favourite meals, using the children's portraits in the columns.

- Draw out a binary tree on the floor, on which the children have to follow the branches according to the object or card in their hand.

- Let the children make simple 'clue books' to identify objects such as leaves, birds, animals.

- Make a card index for information about ourselves, dinosaurs, transport or whatever, in which the children discuss the headings needed and fill in the cards appropriately. These can then be put in a shoe box and left out with various sorting and searching challenges for the children.

There is a multitude of ideas for these types of activity, none of which needs a computer, but all reinforce the processes of information handling. This preparation is important, not only in providing an understanding of 'what's going on', but also in allowing the children to see the advantages of the computer's speed and storage capacity. For some children, typing in details on the screen to set up a database and then seeing a bar chart printed out can be a remote and bewildering activity. A group of year 5 children were baffled when they designed a database of 2D and 3D shapes in Junior Pinpoint which then displayed graphs of their data. They had thought that they had been word processing and could not think how the computer could 'reorganize' their data sheets. Others, who have had some experience of trying to organize, store and search information with other methods, will be delighted to see the speed with which the computer can do the same task.

At the end of an enquiry children need to have the opportunity to discuss the nature of the information they have collected and found and whether their interpretations are valid, relating to the original question. A useful and enjoyable activity to illustrate the variety of ways in which information is presented, altered, filtered and re-presented is to simulate a newsroom. There are several software packages, such as Teletype, Extra ! and Simtex, that simulate a Teletype machine on which news items from reporters and news agencies are generated every few minutes over a set period. The 'news' can be anything from the stealing of the Queen's tarts to a bomb blast in Hyde Park. The children receiving the messages in the 'newsroom' have to decide how to present them by a given deadline in a radio bulletin, TV news item or newspaper format. As well as the elements of role-play and team work in the activity, the children have to consider how they should decide to present the story to a particular audience, how to resolve conflicting reports and choose what to focus on, and what to discard under pressure. This can lead to interesting discussions of the authority of the presentation of information and the ways in which it can be distorted.

Jean Underwood has argued the case for using data handling in the classroom and described the conditions under which the activities are likely to be effective:

- the activity is clearly defined, purposeful and meaningful in the learner's eyes
- the learner has developed a mental map of the database ... the structure of the file is transparent to the user
- graphing tools provide meaningful representations of the data

(Underwood, 1994, p. 87)

There is tremendous potential for IT to support the development of information-handling skills in activities that have purpose and clear learning objectives, engaging the children's interest and encouraging them to develop new skills, concepts and knowledge. IT capability delivered for its own sake can be trivial and sterile. Primary classrooms will soon have access to vast amounts of information on CD ROMs and through networks linking schools with the outside world. Preparing children to be able to work and interact with all this information is an increasingly important part of a teacher's work. The ability to ask relevant and powerful questions, test hypotheses, browse, and explore possibilities for making connections with information to form new knowledge will be required whatever forms the technology takes.

Skills of handling information and understanding its organization and presentation are not confined to 'information technology'. They underpin the ability to make connections between and analyse information in all forms. The demands of our 'information society' are such that people need to have confidence in their abilities to access and make use of information.

IT contributes to the development of these skills by storing, processing and presenting large amounts of data with speed and flexibility. It can perform the tedious tasks, providing the opportunity for children to engage in higher-order skills of identifying good questions, organizing, interpreting and communicating information. The software packages available for use in the classroom provide a variety of models of organizing and interrogating information, and increasingly children will be able to use large databases compiled by specialists in particular areas. As the availability of and access to this wealth of sources widens, the development of skills may focus more closely on effective recognition of salient items, searching and retrieval whilst browsing through vast stores of information.

CHAPTER 4

Using IT to Model, Control and Monitor the World

'What would happen if ...?'

The National Curriculum identifies 'controlling, monitoring and modelling' as distinct ways of working with IT – ways which reflect powerful applications of IT in the everyday world, and which require an investigative approach to solving problems. There is a progression from KS1 to KS2 in that the experiences are developed from a focus on controlling and modelling to include opportunities for monitoring external events with IT, areas which are now accessible to young children because of developments in technology which enable them to focus on the task itself and not the technicalities.

Such ways of working with IT open up broad and exciting areas, encompassing diverse activities such as simulating archaeological digs, making decisions in a Formula One racing team, monitoring changes in the light and temperature of the room, controlling light, sound and movement in working models, and exploring the possibilities of programming 'robots'. Underlying all these activities is the opportunity to ask the question, 'What would happen if ...?', to make some decisions and to see the consequences of those actions in real and imaginary situations. Through these activities children's learning can be supported by the experience of approaching a problem through trial and error, experimentation, observation and the refinement of ideas.

Why is it important to ask that question?

The learning theories which have influenced primary classrooms in the last thirty years have been those which have focused on the importance of interaction in children's learning – interaction with the world outside through physical contact

69

and activities, and interaction with others through communication and language.

Piaget spoke of the development of logical structures in children's thinking which were 'constructed' through action. In the early stages of the child's learning these 'structures' or 'schemata' were limited and qualitatively different from those of mature thinkers. They were altered and updated as the child experienced more of the world and needed more complex models to interpret and explain what was going on. It was through interaction, play and movement in the world outside, encountering new situations which did not 'fit' previous explanations, that children developed flexible systems of symbolic and abstract structures.

The socio-cultural work of Vygotsky (1978), developed by workers such as Jerome Bruner (1986) and Margaret Donaldson (1978), also focused on action and problem solving in learning, but highlighted the importance of language and communication with others, both peers and adults. The child does not construct mental models of the world in isolation, but develops processes and ways of thinking by interaction with and instruction from others. When explanations do not work and experiences do not fit, new models can be developed by turning to others for help in representing these new ideas. Instead of learning everything by discovery, completely from scratch, children learn in a cultural context in which ideas, tips and support are given to help make sense of the world and provide continuity in communities. Although Piaget's theoretical approach emphasized structures built by the experiences of the individual, and Bruner emphasized ways of thinking and instruction, both stress that 'abstract thinking grows out of material actions' (Wood, 1988, p. 9). David Wood commented on the definite evolutionary advantage of internalized representations of the world in the potential ability to think before we act!

Good learners are those who are able to interact with physical and social experiences in the world, aware of puzzlement, deliberation and reflection, in order to gain increasing control over their mental life, and ultimately independence of thought (Grieve and Hughes, 1990). Being able to ask the question, 'What would happen if I did this?', make a prediction, observe the consequences, and adjust the mental model in order to explain the outcomes is a powerful approach to learning. Having confidence in trying out new situations and learning from them in order to move forward in knowledge and understanding should be the foundation for everyone's experience of learning, whether it be through play or for a PhD.

This active questioning approach to learning is included in the 'revelatory' and 'conjectural' paradigms described in the first chapter. Revelatory learning experiences occur when the learner is working with a model in which the rules and relationships are already determined, but need to be explored and pieced together in order to reach an understanding of what is actually going on. Various ideas and explanations have to be tried to see which fit the model and which have to be abandoned as redundant or unhelpful. James Watson and Francis Crick determined the model of the structure of DNA by literally piecing together fragments of knowledge and speculation from scientists' work. They devised some bizarre and improbable suggestions on the way, but by testing and trying their model they eventually found the 'best fit' – and won the Nobel Prize.

The conjectural paradigm for learning experiences is more open-ended. Instead of exploring a predetermined model, the question 'What would happen if ...?' is applied to new situations in order to investigate new possibilities. The rules and relationships in the model are set up by the learner in order to investigate how they develop. At a simple level, setting up a model train set using units of straight and curved track can lead to a vast number of possible track layouts constrained only by other, often more powerful, members of the household. At the other end of the scale, so to speak, jazz improvisation takes a number of rules of harmony and rhythm, works within them, bends them and breaks them in order to produce an interpretation unique to the musician.

Our fast-changing, technological society requires individuals who can adopt this approach to learning through experience and investigation; who have a positive approach to problem solving, flexibility and transferability in new situations. 'Real' scientists, geographers, athletes, mathematicians, historians, artists, photographers, musicians and mountain climbers are

71

able to be in control and participate in situations, make hypotheses about what is going on and test them, and explore new possibilities in order to extend their understanding of the new and unpredictable.

What does IT bring to this approach?

It is argued that IT can enhance and extend not only children's ability to carry out physical activities, but also children's cognitive skills (Papert, 1980, 1993; Underwood and Underwood, 1990; Scaife and Wellington, 1993). IT can be used to simulate physical activities which would be difficult or inaccessible, such as learning to fly an aircraft or operate a nuclear reactor. It can also be used to measure and record physical events which might be tricky for children to do themselves, such as remotely sensing changes in temperature and light in the school playground over 72 hours. Such simulations and applications enable the children to investigate 'What would happen if ... ?' in a safe environment supporting trial and error, experimentation and observation.

IT can also be used to provide opportunities to demonstrate and develop cognitive skills and mental structures. Approaches to problem solving and the expression of mathematical ideas can be explored using the programming language Logo. The following sections will focus on the ways in which IT can be used to extend children's experience in modelling real and imaginary situations, in controlling and measuring events with IT, and in investigations and problem solving with Logo.

Using IT to extend experience in modelling real and imaginary situations

ADVENTURE GAMES AND SIMULATIONS

Games, adventures and simulations enable the children to participate in activities which, although at present constrained by the screen and keyboard, can represent a wealth of worlds for exploration, from rain forests to racing tracks. The development of multimedia representation with CD ROM, interactive video, networks for communication and virtual reality is bringing an abundance of imagery, in both quality and quantity. There are, of course, social implications associated with these developments, particularly in the growth of violent games and access to computer pornography, which may extend children's experience in ways we would not always wish for them.

'Educational' computer games for young children can play an important role in supporting their concentration, group work and motivation. They can be involved in activities choosing clothes to dress a teddy; moving bones to make up a skeleton; giving instructions to lift an elephant onto a truck and drive it off; or moving through a house to look for a hidden mouse. There are many of these games produced for early-years children, most involving discussion, prediction, decision-making, control of a concept keyboard or mouse, observation, and reaction to feedback from the computer. The visual presentation and amount and difficulty of text can vary, and they are usually fun and motivating, using the computer's facilities for speed, graphics, patience and interaction.

Adventure games set up an imaginary world with characters, events, problems to be solved and usually a sense of direction, purpose or 'quest', often finding lost items such as princesses, professors or the king's medicine. As the children move through the adventure, they can record or map their movements and decisions in order to build up the model or representation of the 'world'. It is interesting to see how these representations of the journey develop, from scribbled comments, notes and lines to carefully drawn maps showing connections and scale. 'Educational' adventure games usually set some worthy task to be solved at decision points before the player can move on – finding hidden passwords in a picture, matching shapes to make a key, exploring the Fibonacci series to find a telephone number, or translating pentominoes to mend a gap in a bridge – all requiring discussion or deliberation, and sometimes working away from the computer using other resources, to solve the problem.

The games and adventure games all provide an imaginary and playful context in which to try out decisions and see what would happen if Teddy's trousers were put on before his socks, Jumbo the elephant was lifted before the truck was ready, or the door to the north was opened rather than the door to the east. If an inappropriate or disastrous decision is made, no harm is done other than having to start the game again – more wisely.

Simulations provide models of more realistic situations which can be manipulated and explored. In the adult world, simulations are used to train aircraft pilots, assist doctors in diagnosis of symptoms, model economic situations, and provide 'virtual reality' experiences of driving through the Channel Tunnel. The advantages of using IT to simulate 'real life' are apparent in several aspects of the activity. Safety is a key factor, in enabling dangerous or inaccessible situations to be represented on a screen, either visually or in numbers and words. Diving to salvage a wrecked Tudor warship, learning to fly an aircraft, or landing on the moon can be represented in a classroom quite easily. Similarly, situations remote in space and time can be simulated, enabling the children to travel back in time to see Romans on Hadrian's Wall or have conversations with Egyptian priests to help them identify an object found in an archaeological dig.

Costs can be kept down in the simulation of experiments requiring expensive equipment or resources, and time can be saved in observing the consequences of decisions which could normally take some years to take effect. Children could therefore participate in the simulation of nutrient experiments with plants to investigate the effects of different conditions over four seasons; or take part in the management of a nature reserve and see the consequences of flooding the marshes to provide watersport facilities. As well as saving costs and time, it is possible to give the children the opportunity to see the effects of single or combinations of events which would be difficult to disentangle in real life. The water-sports facilities may provide income to run the nature reserve but have a disastrous impact on the wildlife of the marshes. The computer's speed of processing, graphical display, interaction and presentation all combine to provide an ideal tool for the feedback required to learn from a simulation.

Scaife and Wellington (1993) warn against the dangers of

simulations in the hidden messages that they might convey. In real life, variables cannot often be controlled easily, equally and independently, and the model of reality on which the simulation is based may be incomplete, misleading or even incorrect. It may be necessary to question the validity of the rules and modify the assumptions underlying the relationships in the model. The authority ascribed to the world created by the programmer may be unwarranted but unchallenged (Turkle, 1984; Weizenbaum, 1984).

SPREADSHEETS

Simulations and adventure games are examples of predetermined models in which the rules are 'revealed' by exploration and prediction and pieced together to make a working model which 'fits', providing a more complete picture and explanation for what is going on. It is also possible to use IT applications which enable the users to determine their own relationships in the model, see the consequences of these rules and alter them accordingly to solve particular problems. Spreadsheets are very useful for demonstrating this type of modelling, although the setting up and operating of them can be complicated and more suited to work with older children.

Spreadsheets can be set up with headings, data and formulae in place in order to let the children see the effects of particular changes and comparisons. There are many examples of commercially prepared files providing demonstrations of the use of spreadsheets: investigating the characteristics of the solar system, comparing costs of living in Victorian and modern times, or demonstrating properties of the periodic table. The data and formulae used to express the relationships have already been inserted and sometimes protected from change, but enable the children to see the effects of different elements of the spreadsheet on each other and graphically represent the relationships between them.

It is also possible for the children to think about ways of representing relationships and effects by setting up their own sheets. Planning a school trip may involve costs related to entrance fees, quotations given by different coach companies, catering costs and the number of children involved. It may be necessary to decide on a maximum and minimum number, beyond which the trip would not be viable. Establishing the model for the spreadsheet would involve considering how to express relationships of adding, multiplication, subtraction and division, organizing the layout of the sheet and seeing the effects of different variables, such as, 'How much would it cost if we took thirty-five children?' 'Would it be better value for money if we took seventy?' 'What would be the ratio of children to adults?' and 'Could we afford to have a chocolate biscuit in the packed lunch if we took the cheapest transport?'

Using IT to extend experience in controlling and monitoring events

CONTROL TECHNOLOGY

Children need to be aware of the ways in which IT controls activity in everyday life. They can follow 'technology trails' through the house, from the fridge light switching on as the door opens to the regulation of the washing machine and the programming of the video. They can walk down the high street and see IT controlling the cash dispensers, the car-park barriers and the traffic-light controls. They can play with programmable toys, from buggies to robots, and set off the car alarm – with little difficulty and great glee. This awareness of the ways in which IT can be used to sense what is happening in the environment and initiate some action is an important experience for the children. It provides them with a context in which to work with IT themselves in developing sequences of instructions in order to solve problems of sensing and controlling their own events.

Control technology in the classroom is characterized by the children using a microcomputer to control the switching on and off of lights, buzzers and motors, which can be linked to working models such as traffic control, fairground games and the ever popular burglar detectors. A control technology system consists of the *computer*, which follows instructions given in a *control language* and communicates with an *interface unit*, or buffer box, attached to the computer. This sends signals *out* to the lights, buzzers and motors (output) and receives signals *in* from sensors (input), detecting changes in the immediate environment such as light, temperature, movement, pressure and magnetic fields.

The development of IT capability through control technology focuses on the children giving precise instructions or commands in order to produce a variety of outcomes. These instructions can be simple and direct, or developed into a sequence which the computer can store to be modified and developed as required. Thus it is possible to approach a problem, from directing a 'robot' around an obstacle to operating an automatic barrier in a car park, by asking 'What would happen if ... I gave these instructions?', observing the consequences, and modifying the instructions if necessary.

Young children can experience preliminary controlling activities in playing with programmable 'robots' such as Roamer or Pip. These are devices which will respond to specific commands, either singly or in a sequence, that direct movement over distance and through turn. It is possible, therefore, to instruct Roamer to go forward three 'steps' or units, turn through 90 degrees to the left, go backward six units, turn through 180 degrees to the right and then play a little tune. The advantage of using these devices with children of all ages is that the sequences of instructions are so closely related to their own body movements in space, and are therefore easy to predict and think about when the consequences of the instructions are observed. Roamer can be instructed to move around an obstacle course, go under the table, dance around the corridor and visit the head teacher's office – decorated and modified with Lego bricks and models, to represent animals, buggies and mythical beasts. If Roamer ends up banging into the wastepaper basket instead of going out of the door, is it Roamer's disobedience or an inappropriate instruction in the sequence? The questions 'Why did that happen?' and 'What would happen if ...' are central to this sort of activity.

Robot 'floor turtles' are devices which are given commands through the control language on the computer, communicating either directly through a cable or by an infra-red beam. These turtles are very precise instruments, moving accurately and leaving clear trails if a pen is attached. The language, which is often a form of the Logo language, can also be used to control a 'screen turtle' which moves about the computer screen instead of the floor. The potential for investigation and the development of cognitive skills using Logo will be discussed in further detail in the next section.

Using control technology to develop working models is a challenging experience for the children. Obviously they enjoy making lights flash, buzzers buzz and motors whizz around in various sequences, but the excitement in this work comes when it is applied to a more meaningful context. These sensors and output devices can be incorporated into working models, so that the lighthouse light flashes on and off; the traffic lights work in sequence when the button is pressed at the pelican crossing; the burglar stepping on the pressure pad outside the house is greeted by an alarm of buzzers and lights; the buggy car passing the magnetic switch triggers the motor which turns the gears to open the garage door; the doll being placed in the deck chair will be served a cool drink on a moving trolley and then tipped into the swimming pool; and the footstep of an intruder to the castle tilts a switch which sets off a sequence of instructions to turn motors to raise the portcullis and wheel out the dragons – switching on the tape recording of loud roars and smoke-filled coughs on the way. There is no end to the children's inventiveness in extending their model making and developing the question 'What would happen if ...?', observing the results and refining their ideas to solve the problem.

Control technology offers the opportunity for an investigative approach to solving problems and a development in the complexity of giving and modifying instructions. It also offers the chance for children to engage in processes which they can relate to the real world. They can learn the importance of testing systems to make them foolproof in all circumstances – procedures essential to designers and engineers. They can learn how to collaborate with each other and build on the ideas and insights of the individuals in the group. They can learn the fallibility of the computer and the programmer and the contribution each makes to the situation, developing 'an awareness that whilst the computer might possess superior abilities in terms of patience and exactness, it was they who had the imagination to "see patterns" and actually find solutions to their problems' (Whalley, 1994, p. 148).

They can also learn that the teacher can adopt a new role as consultant, technician, project manager, assessor and evaluator. Rather than giving facts and solutions, the teacher can encourage problem solving in a physical and open-ended situation, providing resources and help with technical expertise when required, instructing in new techniques, questioning and explaining, and developing 'skilful neglect', as described by Beverley Labbett (1988), in letting the children define the problems and work out the solutions through trial and error, description and discussion.

Developing control technology in the classroom is quite a complicated task for the teacher. The equipment required – computer, control software, interface, sensors and output devices – is becoming more user-friendly in design, making the technical aspects of setting up the activities more straightforward. The structure of the control languages used can be complex, the need for knowledge of the syntax getting in the way of the task itself. There are new developments in more visual ways to present the language, using 'object-oriented' software which enables the user to set up the different elements or 'actors' in the task and see them working or 'performing' simultaneously, providing feedback to each other in order to maintain the activity.

These aspects need time and commitment from the teacher to become familiar and confident with the resources in order to support and encourage the children in a busy classroom with many other demands. The nature of the group work should include opportunities for the children to work independently of the teacher, using her or him as a consultant when necessary, to work collaboratively with other children and to work as an individual making contributions to the group. The context in which the activities are presented should be sensitive to the needs and interests of the girls and the boys in the groups. IT can often be seen as a male domain which is off-putting to girls, and Whalley (1992) indicated the importance of an interesting and engaging context to enable girls to demonstrate higher-level thinking in a task using materials with which they may not be familiar. They, however, are often more prepared to work co-operatively than boys, who are more competitive and prone to 'turn taking' which is not as conducive to effective collaborative work.

Despite these cautions, becoming familiar with new learning resources and thinking carefully about planning children's experiences should be central to the teacher's work! As the IT equipment becomes more flexible, accessible and 'transparent' to the task, the time taken to become confident in new areas will be amply rewarded by the quality of the children's ingenuity, imagination and application.

In all these developments, however, it is important that the use of control technology is purposeful and that the children have time to work with quality and accuracy. Anita Straker (1989) emphasized the need for purpose: not to make models for model making's sake, but to take the opportunity to explore construction techniques, investigate properties of materials, illustrate or represent ideas such as gears, buoyancy, transmission of power or electricity, or solve a particular problem. The use of IT to control events should be appropriate. One teacher was puzzled by the enthusiasm of an IT advisory teacher for controlling the movement of a working model with the computer: 'But it's a windmill!'

MONITORING EXTERNAL EVENTS

As well as being able to sense data from the environment in order to control other events, it is also possible to use sensors to monitor and present information about external events. The rather curious term, 'datalogging', is used to describe the process of collecting data from the environment by means of sensors which respond to stimuli such as temperature, light, movement, magnetic fields, electrical current and ultra-violet radiation. The 'response' is in the form of an electrical signal sent to the interface unit, which translates that signal into digital form to be processed by the computer. Analogue data, such as temperature, and digital data, such as a light being on or off, can be processed and presented in this way. The 'sensing unit' can be separate from the computer, storing the data until required; it can also be linked to a portable computer such as a laptop or palmtop or connected directly to a desktop computer with a large screen and printer for presentation. Having the datalogging device separate from the cumbersome desktop computer has the great advantage of being able to take it to the environment – the playground, a field, a corridor or a wardrobe.

The unique contribution of IT to collecting and analysing such information is the speed with which large amounts of data can be monitored, stored and presented in an accessible graphical form for interpretation. The children are therefore able to use the graphs and visual representations of the data as the starting point for the discussion about what is happening, in order to 'tell the story' behind the information shown.

A variety of questions could be asked and experiments set up to monitor data in order to observe what happens and test hypotheses:

- *Which materials are best for keeping warm in winter?* Notice the patterns of temperature change in a line graph produced by a sensor left in a jug of warm water wrapped in fabrics with different insulating properties.

- *Which are the most efficient sunblocks for keeping out UV light?* Note the pattern of values shown by a UV sensor covered in glass smeared in different sunblock creams.

- *Does the sun make the playground hot? Is there a connection between sunlight and temperature?* Leave temperature and light sensors logging data over a 24-hour period and represent the changes in line graphs to note any similar or varying patterns.

- *Which is the coldest part of the night?* Leave the temperature sensor out in the playground overnight and plot a graph of temperature against time.

- *Does the sun rise at different times during the year?* Leave the light sensor out overnight over long periods of time throughout the year to note any patterns in the representation of sunrise. How could 'sunrise' be represented clearly?

81

The advantages of using a computer to store and process the data collected in these investigations are described by Scaife and Wellington (1993, p. 61):

Speed	The computer can log signals much more quickly than human beings, and certainly more quickly than a child with a stop watch, counter and clip board.
Memory	Large amounts of data can be stored and accessed on discs.
Perseverance	Computers do not get bored or hungry logging information consistently over periods of time.
Communication of meaning	The data can be processed and presented in a variety of ways, particularly in an animated, graphical form to show changes over time.
Stimulating	Children show motivation, stimulation and curiosity in working with IT that can be used to encourage further investigation.

The area of datalogging is one in which the technology opens up new possibilities for investigation with 'real data' collected by the children in response to real questions. Children can design experiments to test their hypotheses, observe the outcomes, consider appropriate ways to present the data for interpretation, and think of appropriate methods to communicate their findings to different audiences – from line graphs to story telling. Seymour Papert (1993) describes the 'Kidnet' scheme, supported by the National Geographical Society, in which children are involved in the 'serious work' of collecting data about acid rain and sharing the information through the network to a central computer, which integrates the data and returns it to the participating schools, where the children can analyse and work with it. They discuss the data in the context of global issues and use their expertise in involvement in local environmental campaigns. Children are given the freedom to interpret the events being represented, rather than being burdened with the laborious and often difficult task of collecting the data.

It is this freedom, however, that offers challenges to the teacher in effectively enabling the children to work in open-ended situations. Children should have the opportunity to develop their skills of discussion, negotiation, planning, observation and interpretation as well as social skills of sharing ideas and tolerating others. It is important therefore that the teacher understands the role that IT plays in these situations – as a data-logger and presenter – and understands the role that she or he plays in providing the framework for the children to engage with higher-order skills.

Using IT to extend experience of investigation and problem solving with Logo

The world of Logo, the philosophy behind it, and the activities associated with it are firmly based upon the conjectural paradigm for learning, asking the question, 'What would happen if ...?' in order to learn through action, experience and reflection.

There are many claims made for Logo as 'a language for learning how to think' (Harvey, 1984, p. 21). It is described as a language which allows learners to describe their ways of thinking and the strategies they employ to solve problems. They are able to reflect upon their learning and become 'epistemologists' – scientists of the nature of knowledge. Logo enables children to explore and demonstrate intellectual structures which could not be easily expressed in other ways, and develops an open-ended approach to problem solving, in depth and breadth, which can transfer to other areas of learning.

Some would argue strongly with these claims, particularly in the evidence for transferability of problem-solving skills and in the implementation of these ideas in a busy classroom. However, the debate does raise very interesting questions about teaching and learning through problem solving.

WHAT IS LOGO?

Logo is a programming language developed by a man called

Seymour Papert, based at the Massachusetts Institute of Technology. He was working in the area of artificial intelligence – the concrete description of abstract ideas – from a background of a Piagetian approach to learning (active construction of intellectual structures). His influential book *Mindstorms*, published in 1980, and his recent book *The Children's Machine*, published in 1993, are worth careful consideration in that, being accessible and controversial, they express Papert's developed theory about the role of the computer in education in terms of epistemology, learning and thinking.

He relates his own way of thinking as a child to the Piagetian ideas of the development and change of mental models in the growth of personal knowledge. His own childhood interest in cars and car parts led to his development of sophisticated mental models of gears to explain numbers and relationships, his intellectual structures being directly related to his own active experience. He is committed to the notion that children develop intellectual structures by interaction both with the environment and with the 'learning culture' in which they are working; and he expresses strongly his feeling that schools fail because the learning culture is not related to the children's own experience and the mental models that they have already developed.

He states his interest in extending Piaget's work by encouraging 'intellectual structures that *could* develop as opposed to those that actually at present do develop in the child, and the *design of learning environments* that are resonant with them' (1980, p. 161). He draws on the field of artificial intelligence by claiming that computers provide rich materials to express ideas, making concepts simple and concrete, providing 'objects to think with', and developing a different culture for learning:

> My goal became to strive to create an environment in which all children – whatever their culture, gender, or personality – could learn algebra and geometry and spelling and history in ways more like the informal learning of the unschooled toddler or the exceptional child than the educational process followed in schools.
>
> (1993, p. 13)

The programming language Logo was therefore developed to be an 'object to think with' which would have the characteristics which reflected Papert's view of learning. Richard Noss described these features as 'natural, extensible and procedural' (1983, p. 7).

Logo is natural. It is easy to use and based upon children's own experience of their body movement in space. It was initially related to primitive commands which would direct a floor robot or turtle around the room: moving forward and backward, turning left and right. These turtles were the precursors of the programmable toys Roamer and Pip discussed in the section above. Therefore a sequence such as FORWARD 3 LEFT 60 would make the turtle move three 'turtle units' and turn through 60 degrees to the left. It is also interactive in that it is possible to give direct instructions to the computer in the Logo language, such as FORWARD 5, and see an immediate response, either from the floor turtle or from the representation of the screen turtle.

Logo is extensible. It is built up by the learners as they get to grips with it at their own pace in their own style, rather as young children build up Lego bricks. The principles underlying the simple instructions used by young children to move the turtle can be developed at all intellectual levels, and Logo is used to teach mathematical ideas to physics undergraduates in the same open-ended and exploratory way.

Logo is procedural. The list of primitive commands can be linked together and named and Logo taught a new 'word'. These words or procedures can then be linked together as sub-procedures in other new words. For example, the sequence LEFT 45 RIGHT 90 LEFT 45 would make the turtle turn to the left, to the right and then face the front again. This could be taught as a new word, 'Shimmy':

```
TO SHIMMY
LEFT 45
RIGHT 90
LEFT 45
END
```

When the word SHIMMY was entered, the turtle would follow all the instructions without them having to be typed in separately. This procedure could then be used in another called 'Step':

```
TO STEP
FORWARD 3
SHIMMY
BACKWARD 3
SHIMMY
END
```

and then made into a 'dance' in which the step is repeated five times:

```
TO DANCE
REPEAT 5 [STEP]
END
```

This power to define procedures is a most important characteristic of the language. In problem solving, the general ability to break down the problem into its component parts is very powerful. Papert call this working with 'mind-sized bites', and in the procedure to make the turtle dance, the instructions were broken down into the elements of the 'shimmy' and 'step' and repetitive 'dance'. Any mistakes or unexpected moves can be 'debugged' or identified and altered quite easily by looking closely at the elements of the sequence to see which ones need to be changed. This again is a powerful problem-solving technique: identifying errors in a solution and learning from them. Papert likens these processes of defining 'mind-sized bites' and 'debugging' to playing with 'mental mud pies', encountering and developing intellectual structures by exploring the interactions and effects, just as young children discover the relationships in the physical world by playing with real materials.

LOGO IN THE CLASSROOM

Logo is often introduced to the classroom through indepen-

dent Roamers and Pips or floor turtles attached to the computer. Commands can be entered directly to explore the
immediate possibilities of movement. These can then be
'taught' or stored as sequences to be tested and modified, the
trails of the 'turtles' being recorded by pens inserted under-
neath the device if required. These were discussed in the
section above on control technology, but the processes involved
are those of investigation and modelling.

The 'screen turtle' will also leave a trace of its movements and
can therefore be used to explore specific shapes and patterns.
The children can use FORWARD, BACKWARD, LEFT and
RIGHT as simple commands, or 'primitives', in a sequence to
produce straightforward zig-zags or complicated snowflakes. It
is important, however, that the children are able to relate the
'up' and 'down' on screen to the 'forward' and 'backward' of
their own movements. They are often seen twisting and moving
from side to side to help them predict the turtle's movement in
relation to their own. It can be useful to have fixed on the wall
near the computer a large cardboard 'Turn Turtle', decorated
and marked with 'Left' and 'Right' on its flippers, to spin in the
direction of the screen turtle in order to help out with orienta-
tion on a vertical plane.

It can take a great number of commands to draw a particular
shape and it is often more efficient to break down the long list
into procedures of 'building blocks' as in the 'Dance' made up
of a 'Step' and a 'Shimmy'. Rajender, an 11-year-old boy, was
drawing a firework which took 40 commands when typed directly into the computer. By breaking down the plans into
procedures for 'body', 'top', 'stick' and 'flames' he was able to
assemble the larger procedure for the 'firework' from the sub-
procedures, spotting the areas for debugging more easily. Other
children investigated ways of drawing cats, trucks, chrysanthe-
mums, spirals, regular polygons, windmills and circles.
Whenever they were puzzled, they 'walked turtle' and tried to
trace out the desired shape themselves as they walked around,
following their directions in English – 'forward one step, left a
little bit, lots of times' – and translating them into Logo,
REPEAT 500 [FD 1, LT 1]. (What would this draw and how
could it be modified?)

Keeping Logo notebooks, either as individuals or in working groups, is a good way to see the development of plans and ideas. Keeping them notionally 'secret' is also a good way of ensuring 'playground transmission' of ideas and tips. It was interesting to see how quickly the word got around that the code for the turn in a pentagon was 72!

Exploration with variables and algebra can be very exciting, arising from the context of the children's ideas. Year 1 children had used the floor turtle to draw a chair using lines and right angles. They decided that they wanted to make it into Daddy Bear's chair, and could they draw a medium and small-size chair for Mummy and Baby? This led into a discussion, in their own terms, of a general procedure to draw a chair and the variable size of the lengths of the lines. Similar investigations in a year 6 class produced a procedure to draw a spiral based on any regular polygon, by defining a variable for the number of sides and relating that to the angle which would need to be turned within the spiral. The challenge had arisen from a question, 'Can we draw a snail shell of any shape we choose?', which had taxed the children and the teacher, but led to rowdy cheers when solved!

Such an open-ended way of working can be very demanding and very rewarding for all involved. Beryl Maxwell, a teacher who used Logo extensively in her class, summarized her experiences: 'The Logo environment provides an atmosphere, where they are not frightened to communicate their thinking, be it right or wrong, because they accept that wrong answers can be helpful in their learning' (1984, p.106).

Three different aspects of using Logo were described by Anita Straker (1989):

1 It can encourage discovery learning in the balance between free activity and guidance in progression and development.

2 It can help children develop mathematical concepts such as big and small numbers, positive and negative numbers, number operations, distance, angles, estimation, properties of 2D shapes, line and rotational symmetry, translation, tessellation, co-ordinates, algebra, speed and direction.

3 It can provide insight into the power of programming, relating closely to general problem-solving skills of analysing the problem, devising a plan, executing the plan and reviewing or debugging it.

A WORD OF CAUTION

The claims made for Logo and the potential it has for developing thinking and representing strategies for problem solving are bold, and many teachers and children have worked with great enthusiasm and confidence in the open-ended and conjectural way it encourages. There is, however, little empirical evidence of the success of Logo in being able to guarantee the transfer of general problem-solving abilities. True Logo enthusiasts would claim that the quality of learning brought about by Logo is not of the nature to be measured in empirical tests, but the debate is important, as it raises essential issues for classroom teachers.

Jean and Geoffrey Underwood (1990) reviewed a number of studies which looked at the types of improvement in cognitive skills that could be attributed to children's experience with Logo. Klahr and Carver (1988) demonstrated successful transfer of debugging skills to other problems after working with Logo. Clements and Gullo (1984) showed developments in creative thinking in a Logo group, and Helen Finlayson (1984) noted the benefits of Logo experience in children being able to explain underlying rules in a separate problem.

These improvements in the 'cognitive toolkit' do not, however, map directly onto the claims made for Logo in rigorous thinking, abstract mathematical concepts, heuristics and planning, debugging and metacognition. Some writers, such as Pea (1983), called Papert a 'technoromantic' and claimed that there was no evidence of transfer of high-level skills, indeed likening the arguments for the benefits of Logo to those used in the promotion of the teaching of Latin to improve logical thinking.

Tony Simon (1987) contested the powerful effect of Logo in self-learning by highlighting the difficulties of implementing Piagetian learning in the practical classroom situation. Other researchers have demonstrated effective learning of mathematical models through a structured approach to Logo in the

classroom when the teacher gave very close guidance, supported by specific learning materials (Howe *et al.*, 1979). In fact,
Simon noted that the development of effective, high-level,
general problem-solving skills, such as those demonstrated by
chess grandmasters, took a long period of intensive learning
and practice, a resource not readily available in a classroom with
limited access to Logo on one computer.

THE ROLE OF THE TEACHER IN WORKING WITH LOGO

The role often adopted by teachers working with children using
Logo is one of guide, consultant, questioner and fellow learner.
The skill of learning to 'keep quiet' is encouraged, as children
discuss, deliberate and debug their programs, and the teachers
try to let them be more in control of their own problem-solving
strategies and thinking processes. It could be argued, in fact,
that the positive changes in the children's motivation, willingness to work together and attitude to their problem-solving
tasks could be related as closely to the teacher's change in attitude, role and style of interaction as to the Logo language.
Papert's ideas are very much focused on a theory of learning in
an IT-rich environment, rather than theory of teaching with
limited resources.

Indeed, Hoyles and Sutherland (1989) noted the importance
of the quality of the interaction between children and the teacher
whilst working with Logo. The interaction and intervention
strategies adopted by the teacher were far more subtle than at
first thought. The teacher did not just 'stand back' and let it
happen, but used a variety of questions, prompts, giving and with-
holding of information at different times to support and increase
pupil autonomy and challenge. It is interesting, therefore, to
note the importance of that role in supporting and developing
children's work in an open-ended and conjectural environment.

Having the confidence to ask the question, 'What would
happen if … ?', is an important element in learning, being able
to predict, observe, reflect upon and build on experience. This
approach is rooted in social constructivist theories of learning
and witnessed where children are engaged in action, observation and asking questions.

IT can make a distinctive contribution to this way of working in its ability to simulate or model 'microworlds', which the children can explore safely to reveal the underlying rules and relationships in that 'microworld' – whether it be an imaginary land in an adventure game or a mathematical relationship. IT can also be used to control and monitor events in the outside world, instructed by sequences of commands designed by the children to solve particular problems, from flashing lights in a model lighthouse to setting up a weather station. Logo can provide the opportunity to ask the question 'What would happen if … ?' in an open-ended way in which the outcome cannot always be predicted and the learner can 'think about thinking'. The debate about the effectiveness of Logo continues, but the issues raised for the teacher's roles are challenging.

Underlying all these ways of working is a very important theme related to the contribution of IT to teaching and learning. IT can provide an environment in which the learner is in control and in a position to investigate by asking questions, trying out ideas and watching the consequences. The outcomes of these decisions need not be threatening, physically or psychologically, but lead to further exploration and experience.

CHAPTER 5

IT for All: Empowerment and Limitations

There are areas in the lives and experiences of people in which information technology makes a unique contribution, providing access to levels of communication, amounts of information and modes of expression previously unavailable. There are also areas in which the experiences of groups of people, girls and boys, cultural and socio-economic groups – could either be extended by new ways of working with IT or restricted by the perceptions of the place of IT in our society. These opportunities and perceptions should be understood by teachers in order to make sure that all children, regardless of their special educational needs, gender, race, or socio-economic class, have the opportunity to experience the contribution that IT can make to their learning and ways of working.

Special educational needs

> Information Technology is making a unique and valuable contribution to the learning of pupils with SEN, enriching their learning experiences and enhancing their access to a broad curriculum.
>
> (DES, 1990, p. vii)

One child in every five is likely to receive special education at some point in their schooling. That is, 20 per cent of the population experience learning difficulties of some degree, which cause them to have significantly greater difficulty in learning than their peers. Of this group 2 per cent will require a statement of special educational needs and special provision, as described in the UK Education Act 1981, and may have the National Curriculum modified or disapplied. There are also procedures described in the Code of Practice on the Identification and Assessment of Special Educational Needs for assessing the needs of and providing for the further 18 per cent who do not require 'statements', but do require special educational provision of some sort. Teachers in mainstream classrooms may work with children with a range of learning difficulties – from mild and intermittent difficulties causing children to 'fall behind', to severe physical disability, sensory impairment or emotional difficulties – and they need guidance and support in recognizing and providing for those needs.

David Hawkridge and Tom Vincent explain very clearly the unique contribution that IT can make to the education of children with learning difficulties by highlighting the issues of 'access' and 'magnifying abilities'. IT is able to provide children with access to communication, expression and information, and thus a broader curriculum and experience. It can enable them to share and communicate with others and support their own learning and cognitive development. 'The essential principle we work to is that the technology should be used to magnify abilities that are there, bypassing as much as possible cognitive, emotional, physical and sensory disabilities' (Hawkridge and Vincent, 1992, p. 28).

They emphasize that special educational needs arise from an interaction between three factors:

1 innate human abilities;
2 the conditions under which learning occurs;
3 the nature of the learning task;

and it is the capability of new technologies to alter the conditions of learning and the nature of the task dramatically. These are bold claims, which are not borne out for every person with learning difficulties using IT, but there is a large body of evidence of examples of good practice in which children are able to achieve remarkable success and degrees of confidence in their work. The philosophy which underpins this work for children and teachers is one of empowerment and independence. 'You can become known, in other words, for *who you know you are* rather than for what others have interpreted you to be' (Hawkridge and Vincent, 1992, p. 26).

PHYSICAL DISABILITIES AND SENSORY IMPAIRMENT

Perhaps the most striking examples of access and magnification of abilities are seen with children and adults with severe learning difficulties caused by their physical or sensory disability. Their experience and expression may be constrained by lack of co-ordinated movement, speech, sight or hearing. Adaptations can be made to the technology used by the able-bodied to enable people to input and interact with information in ways more appropriate to their particular needs. The technology can then process and manipulate information in order to produce appropriate output to be communicated and shared with everyone. It is therefore possible to have conversations, both immediate and long-distance; access encyclopaedias and directories; print text and visual images; and collaborate with peers and colleagues like any able-bodied person.

Means of providing input and interaction with the computer can be designed to match an individual's abilities. Keyboards can be produced with different sizes and sensitivity of keys or keyguards to help direct accurate pressing of the keys. Concept keyboards can be used as alternative and flexible keyboards. These flat boards are attached to the computer, which is programmed to respond to a touch on the concept keyboard in certain ways for certain locations. Overlays or membranes can therefore be placed on these keyboards and designed to be suitable for the child and the task. One child may only be able to move his or her arm to press one side or the other of the concept keyboard, which then elicits a particular effect on the computer screen. For example, touching the top of a picture of a bus causes a bus on the screen to be coloured red, touching the door causes windows and doors to be drawn on the screen bus. Others may be able to touch sequences of pictures or text in order to produce a story written by a word processor. Photos taken of the children in the park, for example, could be used to provide a sequence of sentences which describe the day out. Touch screens can also be placed in front of the usual monitor, and the children can interact with the software by pointing directly to areas on the screen.

If co-ordination of movement with adapted keyboards is difficult, other switches more suited to particular needs can control the computer. Arm, foot and hand switches can be used to signal responses and reactions to events on the screen, from games to the scanning of letters to be typed in a word-processed document. Small movements of the head, face and eyes can be detected as switches, as can 'suck and blow' tubes and sound. Speech can be recognized, the computer being programmed to respond to commands given in the user's voice. It is therefore possible for a child having no speech and difficulty in controlling motor co-ordination to use a foot or arm switch to control a portable computer attached to the arm of a wheelchair. Characters can be scanned and selected to build up sentences on the screen in a word processor. The text can be checked and edited before the speech synthesizer is used to communicate the thoughts and ideas to another person. It is possible to prepare some sentences beforehand for more immediate conversation, such as, 'I'd like to say something now' and 'I haven't finished yet!' (Rahamim, 1993, p. 21).

Children with visual impairments can benefit from the facilities for enlargement of text and pictures on screen or print outs. This can be particularly useful for working with visual images, where the children have the opportunity to use the 'zoom' facilities of graphics systems to express their visual imagination. A project at George Orwell school in London, a secondary school in which visually impaired pupils are integrated with mainstream pupils, used the sophisticated Quantel Paintbox system to provide enlargements and colour changes to suit the pupils' particular needs. Such equipment is used by professional production houses and broadcasting companies and is very expensive for an educational budget, but the project planned to develop materials for more accessible IT resources found in many schools (McTaggart, 1994).

One of the most striking advances in new technologies for those with impaired sight is the development of talking books and word processors. Some simple word processors for primary schools have the facility for enlarged and talking text, albeit in a rather 'robotic' voice, which often charms the children by its limitations. CD ROMs have enabled the storage of vast amounts of visual and sound information, which can be read aloud in a more flexible way than a linear audio cassette of a narrative. It is possible to read out selected words and sentences, rather than whole blocks of text, and, using hypertext techniques, provide access through sound to a vast amount of linked information, thus making immediately accessible works such as the *Grolier Encyclopedia*, which would normally take up 21 volumes of printed text and 350 large Braille volumes!

Blind children are able to make use of screen readers, Braille translators, speech synthesizers and 3D representations of diagrams and pictures. It is interesting, though, that the developments in the graphical Windows interfaces for personal computers do limit the use for the visually impaired. There are some developments for screen readers to 'read' the icons, menus and position of the mouse pointer, but the interfaces which are described as 'intuitive' exclude a sizeable sector of the population.

The visual medium does, however, present great advantages to the hearing impaired. The NCET outlined ways in which IT could meet the special educational needs of hearing-impaired children:

At Primary level,

- the development of literacy skills, vocabulary and language extension, with more direct reinforcement of selected aspects than is needed by hearing peers, can be achieved through word processing, with the help of symbol systems and voice synthesis

- improved expression and communication, with enhanced receptive language skills, can occur through the use of age-appropriate listening and reading programs

- improved general cognitive and communication skills can be developed through collaborative decision-making and problem-solving programs, including simulations and adventure games.

(from NCET, 1991a)

Children with hearing difficulties are able to have a world of conversation opened up to them through new technologies. The use of electronic mail with its rapid response and informal style is motivating for children, who can become involved in conversations in which they can see words, phrases and structures in the use of language which would not be easily accessible by signing or lip reading. Fax too provides an immediate form of interaction which can also use diagrams and signs, but an exciting extension of these modes of communication is the videophone. A Telecommunity Project at Frank Barnes Primary School and Oak Lodge Secondary School in London set up videophone links between pupils. They were able to sign to each other and exchange information about each other's schools, something that was particularly important to the primary children, who would have had little opportunity to experience the words and images available to hearing children from conversations with older children and through watching television programmes about school life. The ability to 'chat' with strangers over a distance raised issues of overcoming shyness in social communication and developing confidence in initiating and maintaining communication with a wider audience (McKeown, 1994).

COGNITIVE LEARNING DIFFICULTIES

The group of children with cognitive learning difficulties, whether mild, moderate or severe, is the largest and least served by IT (Hawkridge and Vincent, 1992). It is also the group that may be encountered most often in mainstream classrooms, and the educational needs of these children are met by the collaboration of classroom teachers, parents and special needs co-ordinators, and possibly of external agencies and support. There are many encouraging signs that teachers are using IT in imaginative ways to support these needs and provide access to the curriculum, but there are still felt to be insufficient resources and training.

Standard software used by all the children in the class can be adapted and extended by the use of devices employed effectively with physically and sensorily disabled children to give wider access to resources, experiences and ways of expressing ideas. Talking books on disc or CD ROM provide the opportunity to read and listen to illustrated and interactive stories; talking word processors enable the children to listen to their own work. Concept keyboard overlays or word lists used with a word processor can provide starting points for writing commonly needed words, phrases and sequences. They take away the laborious chore of typing on a keyboard, but provide flexibility for adding the children's own thoughts and ideas as the writing develops. The whole class can be involved in the discussion and stimulus, the overlays being designed by the teacher – and children – at appropriate levels, using words and pictures.

The word processor can be used to present beautifully edited and printed work for children who have only known the discouragement of poor handwriting and grubby, dog-eared paper. Attractive and readable font styles and sizes can be chosen and the format and appearance of a piece of work taken seriously, both for writers and for readers. Spelling checkers and predictive word processors, which attempt to provide a list of possible words after the first few letters have been typed, can reduce the risk of 'getting it wrong' and 'playing safe' by enabling the children to try new words and return to edit spellings later. Children can experience the delight of producing work of high quality, such as a book for younger children, which is admired and used by others, after discussion, editing and praise.

Graphics packages can also offer opportunities to experiment with and present line, colour, pattern and texture in high-quality colour print outs. Children who have poor co-ordination with brushes and paints, and produce results with these which disappoint them, can persevere with a mouse or line tool, erasing mistakes and trying out new possibilities. Their pictures can be enlarged and displayed to encourage them to try other media, knowing that their visual ideas are valued.

The bringing together of speaking, listening, reading and writing in a multisensory way for children with learning difficulties is marvellously illustrated by work with multimedia. Photographs can be taken, pictures drawn, text written, speech and sound effects recorded, and all combined in a collaborative effort requiring planning, structure, negotiation and responsibility. Children in St Peter's Primary School in Belfast used HyperCard on the Apple Macintosh to write, draw pictures and record sound about themselves and their story about winning a trip to Japan, illustrated with examples of clip art and sound effects of their winning names being called and aeroplanes taking off. They worked together to produce the different sections, helping each other out with suggestions in solving problems as they became familiar with the software. They quickly grasped the notion of 'buttons' linking the pages to each other to provide different routes through the story, and were able to set high standards of themselves in solving problems with new features of the package. As their teacher reported, working on the project had become a vehicle for learning about language, team work and their own success:

> I read the last line over and over to myself: 'The teacher looked so proud of us'. I thought this must indeed be a rare feeling for most children with special educational needs, yet one it is natural for them to want.
>
> (Skeffington in Hawkridge and Vincent, 1992, p. 122)

Open-ended work with Logo, in which the children are given the opportunity to work with their own problems and demonstrate their thinking without articulate spoken language, is another remarkable area in which teachers have been able to develop the children's ideas and confidence. Giving commands from the keyboard may be cumbersome and abstract, but the use of Roamers and turtles links the actions and the building up of sequences to the children's own movement and ideas of number, counting, angle, ordering and estimation demonstrated in the 'microworld'. The commands can be displayed on a concept keyboard overlay designed to reflect the children's understanding, from pictures of 'turn' and 'steps' to written words and associated units. The concept keyboard can also be turned to match the direction of the turtle and the child's body position.

Working with IT can provide the same elements of motivation for children with learning difficulties as for anyone else. The computer's animation, feedback, patience and interaction provide a safe and enjoyable experience for the children, and there are many programs written to support language, number and perceptual development. Games which involve recognition of patterns, shapes, colours, letters, numbers and sequences as well as stimulate discussion and problem solving can also promote paired or group work and collaboration which might be artificial in other circumstances.

DYSLEXIA

Dyslexia, considered to be a specific learning difficulty, has been the focus of some attention in terms of the potential of IT to support learning and communication. The characteristics of average or above-average intelligence, difficulties in reading, writing and spelling, sequencing, remembering links between sound and symbol, holding instructions and a degree of motor clumsiness can be addressed in a multisensory way. It is thought that the facility of IT to integrate sight and sound media could be useful in developing resources for children and adults with these difficulties. At first, it was thought that spelling checkers would provide useful support, but in fact users' bizarre and unusual attempts at spelling often produced suggestions for alternative words which were equally bizarre in meaning and lack of context.

Predictive word processors and talking spelling checkers can be useful, if designed to be more subtle and responsive to the individual using them, basing the suggestions for commonly misspelt words on frequently used or required word lists, rather than an all-purpose dictionary. The advantage of the word processor is that it gives the opportunity to 'have a go', with time for rereading, reflection and editing (NCET, 1992a).

EMOTIONAL AND BEHAVIOURAL DIFFICULTIES

A common theme throughout many of the examples of the use of IT with children with special educational needs is the access it gives to work that the children can be proud of and share with others. Nothing succeeds like success, and the confidence that a well-presented story or well-received collaborative effort can give can be the most valuable aspect of this work. Children with challenging behaviour or emotional difficulties can also be reached and given the opportunity to express themselves as individuals or members of a group in ways which were not available to them before and, significantly, have not been associated with poor performance or failure. Mastering IT skills and being able to share those with peers – and teachers – gives children the chance to show their abilities and ideas and take responsibility for helping others (NCET, 1992b).

TEACHERS' NEEDS

Not everything in the garden is rosy, however. There are many examples of 'IT solutions' causing frustration and anxiety because of inappropriate resources or too much faith being put into the IT as the solution, rather than the support it provides for the teacher's work with the child. There is a wide range of abilities and difficulties, which can alter as the child develops. It is therefore essential that the child's needs are accurately assessed in order to provide useful resources. There have been centres set up for the assessment of individual communication needs, such as ACE (Aids to Communications in England), CALL (Communication Aids for Language and Learning) and the collaboration between the Open University and the National Federation of ACCESS Centres.

Teachers need encouragement to build their own confidence with IT in order to be more informed of the possibilities for the children with special needs in their class. They need to have time to practise, keep up to date and keep in touch with other teachers and organizations. Indeed, the HMI Report in 1990, *Education Observed: Information Technology and Special Educational Needs in Schools*, described the situation very clearly:

The development of effective use of IT with individuals or groups

101

of pupils is crucially dependent upon the commitment of individual teachers who require:

- professional and technical INSET
- sufficient equipment for classroom use
- good quality information about IT materials and deployment
- technical assistance and maintenance services.

(DES, 1990, p. vii)

Gender and IT

After considering the encouraging ways in which IT can extend the learning experiences of children with learning difficulties, it is sobering to consider that there is a large group of children being 'put off' IT and computers and consequently being denied access to information and empowerment. Gill Kirkup, in discussing the optimistic and pessimistic approaches to the impact of IT in our society, commented, 'the reality of the "computer revolution" has been that, like all technological innovations, its impact has varied across different categories of people' (Kirkup and Keller, 1992, p. 267).

Celia Hoyles expressed the situation very clearly in *Girls and Computers*:

It is a matter of grave concern that our culture is defining computers as pre-eminently male machines. Despite the fact that in everyday life computers are becoming ubiquitous, the use of the computer in education seems to be following the traditional lines of gender bias in society. The present situation raises distinctly familiar questions of equity in terms of access to and use of technology. While girls and boys might show a similar appreciation of the significance computers might have for their personal futures, boys tend to be more positively disposed than girls towards computers, are more likely than girls to take optional computer courses in school, to report more frequent home use of computers, and tend to dominate the limited computer resources that are available in school. It is also the case that even when girls are able to obtain access to the machines in school, only a restricted set of activities (which exclude programming for example) are often deemed to be appropriate for them. Finally, few girls take up any employment (other than data processing or word processing).

(Hoyles, 1988, p. 1)

This was written in the mid to late 1980s, but the situation in the 1990s does not seem much changed, although there has been some interesting work looking at some of the factors that affect the experiences of girls and produce such negative attitudes.

There is hope that the development of IT applications across the curriculum, and the gradual impact of the National Curriculum requirements for IT capability, will affect the next generation's approach to the potential of IT. In the meantime, there are many students and teachers who have had negative and frustrating experiences with IT, which they must identify and address in order to provide positive and encouraging experiences for the children in their classrooms. Before thinking about the implications for the primary classroom, it is useful to consider the attitudes of students and secondary pupils in order to understand the impact of early experiences on later decisions.

EXPERIENCES OF IT IN SCHOOLING

A survey of students' IT experience on entry to initial teacher education in 1991/2 indicated that there were significant gender differences in the previous use of computers, 10 per cent more males having used IT in some way before starting their course. It was more likely that IT was used in higher education than at school, and although some students had used it in previous employment, the focus had been very narrow and had not provided confidence in using a range of IT applications in teaching. There were also significant gender differences in reported competence in IT, except word processing, and women showed significantly less personal confidence with computers. It was interesting to note, however, that the length of use of IT was a key to improving attitudes for both men and women of all ages, indicating the importance of access – in quantity and quality – in building up confidence and capability (Davis and Coles, in press).

In recent years, the proportion of women entering the IT industry or taking up related courses in higher education, such as computer science, has declined in the United Kingdom. 'The proportion of women entering UK universities to study computer science courses fell from 24 per cent in 1979 to 15 per cent in 1984 and to less than 10 per cent in 1989' (Kirkup and Keller, 1992, p. 269). There has not been a corresponding decrease in the proportion of women entering science and technology courses in physics, chemistry and engineering, which indicates that girls and women entering higher education are choosing *not* to pursue computing courses and have been discouraged by their previous experience of using computers during their years at school (Newton and Beck, 1993).

Bridget Somekh reports that there is no evidence that girls are hesitant in using micros in the early years of the primary school, but they often begin to be hesitant towards the end of the junior school (Somekh, 1988). What is it in the childhood experience of girls and boys, inside and outside school, which seems to cause such a shift in attitude and confidence with IT? Which factors in classroom interactions have such a powerful effect on the possibilities open to children as they grow older and make decisions about their interests, abilities and future studies and employment? What are the issues that teachers need to be aware of and sensitive to in the children's social and cognitive development? There are three possible characteristics of girls and boys which could contribute to the differences observed: ability, attitude and approach.

ABILITY

It has been suggested that girls lack the intellectual abilities to deal with IT, and indeed some girls, when questioned as to why they were not interested, commented, 'It's difficult and complicated ... you feel you need to be a genius' (Newton and Beck, 1993). Girls who achieved similar examination results in computer studies to boys were considered by the teachers to have done so by 'diligence' whilst the boys showed 'flair' (Culley, 1988).

Although reminiscent of the reasons put forward for girls not being fit to receive the same education as boys, due to their smaller brains and hysterical disposition, these arguments do not fit the evidence. Newton and Beck (1993) describe a number of studies which demonstrate the overlap in cognitive abilities of females and males: girls perform at levels superior to boys in some areas of programming, and there are no gender differences in the procedural thinking used in computer programming. Underwood and Underwood (1990) broaden the discussion from 'programming' and state that girls perform at the same level as boys in a variety of computer-related tasks. Culley (1988) also noted that girls in single-sex schools who were encouraged to choose computer-related subjects achieved highly.

The differences do seem to be more related to the effects that attitudes and approach have on the ways in which girls and boys work with IT. The interaction between the children, computer and teacher in the classroom is complex, and teachers need to be sensitive to this in the face of the strength of the images and expectations that children bring into the classroom with them. Somekh noted, 'There is general agreement that girls show as much enthusiasm for computers as boys when their teachers are aware of the potential problems and the school has an effective policy for girls' use of computers' (Somekh, 1988, quoted in Beynon and Mackay, 1993, p. 162).

ATTITUDE

Information technology is generally associated with the 'male domain' by children and adults, which in itself affects the confidence and self-esteem of girls operating in that domain (Griffiths, 1988). Interestingly, girls are less likely to hold extreme stereotypical views and do not consider IT to be 'just for the boys' as much as the boys do (Eastman and Krendl, 1987).

The popular image of new technology has historically been designed and marketed for males. The first 'home computers' were associated with electronic hobbyists and developed into the entertainment and games market, which reflected sports, games and military links with competition, aggression and violence. Many of the 'fantasy' games were also associated with traditionally male 'dungeons and dragons' games, whilst the toy companies promoted My Little Pony and Shopping Mall Madness for the girls. In the business world, the marketing imagery reinforced the status of the men and women involved, men being portrayed as the manager, engineer and powerful decision-maker whilst women sat at keyboards and entered data. The 'hard tech' image that is associated with power and prestige is, in fact, inappropriate in an area which is 'about communication, about interface between people and computers, about organizing information, and about devising new ways to work' (Newton and Beck, 1993, p. 144). Organizations producing materials for schools, such as the Equal Opportunities Commission and NCET, took care to promote more positive images of women using IT, for example in the NCET pack *Why Me? Why IT?* (NCET, 1994c).

How are these attitudes about the nature and domain of IT developed in young children? The culture and jargon of the field, the role models presented by teachers, the access to computers at home, the attitudes of the boys to the girls, and the perceptions of the girls all contribute to the picture that the girls and boys build up of expectations of their place in the world of IT.

The jargon associated with IT can be as baffling, exclusive and unnecessary as jargon in any other field, from cars to cameras. It is particularly important that teachers are aware of the effects of such language on all children's understanding and confidence across the curriculum. The fast-changing world of IT can be perceived as a specialized culture requiring social as well as technical knowledge, as networks and interest groups are set up. These can range widely, from a group of children sharing experiences and expertise in computer games to people with a common interest in 3D chess making connections with each other on the Internet. For children at primary school, games form a key part of an important social network outside school from which girls are often excluded (Culley, 1993).

The role models and attitudes presented by the teachers to

the children are very important. Historically, in the early 1980s, the teachers associated with computers when they were being introduced on a large scale into schools were usually male and, in secondary schools, usually associated with the maths or science department. In the primary sector, even though the proportion of male teachers is smaller than that of female teachers, more men than women teachers attended the IT courses run by the local education authority (Hall and Rhodes, 1988).

There has been considerable broadening of involvement for all teachers since that time, but men and women teachers need to reflect carefully upon the images they might convey to the children. John Beynon (1993b) gives an entertaining, yet alarming, account of a male primary teacher, an ambitious IT enthusiast, referred to by the children as 'Mr Micro'. His approach epitomized a focus on the technology rather than on what was actually happening for the children around the computer, where girls were being bullied by the boys and restricted in their use of the resources and development of their ideas. The children also contribute to the general stereotypes. In my own school in the early 1980s, although I was the IT co-ordinator, if there was a technical problem the children would often suggest 'Shall we call in Mr Green?', even though Mr Green was actually more able than I to help them find a dropped stitch in their knitting and was happy for me to take on the 'technical' role.

Teachers often equate success in computer work with time spent on the computer, rather than understanding of the task. Girls were not observed to spend as much recreation time playing with the computer and exploring the 'power' of the programs and applications, and were considered to have achieved their high grades by diligence in coursework, rather than by the 'flair' attributed to the boys. The girls' access to resources is a crucial factor, particularly as they are often dominated by the 'first come first served' boys in the queue.

Secondary male and female teachers were also noted to have sharply different attitudes about how computers should be used in their schools. Females tended to have a more egalitarian view that IT could be used for all across the curriculum, whilst some males expressed a more elitist view that priority should be given to 'high fliers', particularly boys interested in maths and science (Carter, 1987). It is to be hoped that the National Curriculum requirements for IT capability to be developed across the curriculum in Key Stages 1 and 2 and through focused courses and curriculum subjects in Key Stages 3 and 4 will counteract this attitude!

The access that the children have to computers at home is also an important factor in building up 'technological esteem' and confidence in approaching the resources at school. Although computers for the home market were originally targeted as 'toys for boys', there has been a growth in the purchase of general-purpose personal computers using word processors, graphics and communications as well as games. Unfortunately, when children are asked whom the computers were bought *for*, the reply was 85 per cent boys and 14 per cent girls, even though more of the girls said they wanted a computer (Culley, 1988). It is interesting to ask the children in the class who has a computer at home, who uses it most and in whose bedroom it is kept.

The attitudes of the boys to the girls can be very discouraging. Secondary-school girls described how the boys took over and bragged about their own knowledge. 'Boys seem to take over and show off. We get shoved around by boys at school so rarely get access. Boys think they know everything: they push girls to the side. If girls make mistakes, boys make fun of them' (Newton and Beck, 1993, p. 141). Groundwater-Smith and Crawford (1992) also noted the case of a school in Denmark where the boys were considered to be the 'hosts' of the computer room and the girls the 'guests'.

The battle over the keyboards is by no means restricted to secondary schools. There are many accounts and experiences of mixed groups of girls and boys in a primary classroom, where the boys dominate the keyboard and decision-making and the girls sit passively behind. I observed two boys and a girl in year 3 working with the Roamer. The girl was told that she could write down the instructions whilst the boys programmed the Roamer to move around an obstacle course made of rubber rings. Whenever they made a mistake, they moved the rubber ring, and whenever the girl made a suggestion she was told, 'Be quiet, we're predicting.' She sat excluded and bored throughout the session, murmuring to me, 'It's such a pain, working with boys.'

John Beynon observed a year 4 primary class and described the ways in which the girls complained about the boys interfering by pressing keys on the keyboard, sitting in front, not taking turns and 'slagging off' the girls. One boy when unleashed on the computer changed into a bully, and the girls were bored, frustrated and 'relegated to functionaries' (Beynon, 1993b). There were some observed instances of girls being dominant and fighting back ('Why don't you just have a snooze instead of bossing us around all the time?'), but they were not frequent, and even then the girls often enlisted help from the teacher or another powerful character in the classroom. The perceptions of IT from the girls in this year 4 class were usually positive and related to getting jobs in the future, being able to think things out and having fun. They were also more critical and evaluative about alternative ways of doing a task or solving a problem, and acknowledged anxiety about technical hitches and losing their work.

When secondary girls were questioned about their perceptions of themselves in a computing career they responded with a view of a profession which provided prospects for promotion and good pay, but not very much opportunity to use a range of abilities. They also questioned their own 'cleverness' in being able to get into such a career and expressed doubts about wishing to work in teams dominated by men (Newton and Beck, 1993). Girls in single-sex schools did not seem to have such negative perceptions about themselves and their abilities in computing. In fact, three girls working with Logo commented on the encouragement their teacher had given them to persevere and succeed with a problem:

> Boys are always being encouraged to do special projects and trying new ideas in maths. Most girls just do the work that has been set for them and don't bother to explore new ideas. This is because they haven't enough encouragement. Our teacher praises us every time we do something different. With her encouragement, we could do anything.
>
> (Josie, Lorraine and Sarah, in Hoyles, 1988, p. 18)

The research evidence and anecdotal observations of teacher colleagues paint a rather depressing picture of girls' IT experiences at the end of the twentieth century. It is to be hoped that the changing emphasis in the National Curriculum, and the developments of more powerful computers with accessible interfaces and useful software for communication, handling and investigation of information, will help to make girls and boys more confident about what they can do with IT. Increasing the number of girls wishing to take computer science to a higher level might not be the major battle. It is surely much more important that girls are aware of all the possibilities of using IT in a powerful way, to give them opportunities and choice in what they do, rather than limited and sterotyped experiences and perceptions. Teachers have to be aware of these possibilities in order to give all children access to the world of information. They also have to be aware of how their own experiences, positive and negative, relate to those they provide for the children in the classroom.

APPROACHES

Teachers' and children's assumptions and expectations of girls' and boys' achievements with IT are often based on general cultural images and observed behaviour in the classroom. It is a commonly held belief that girls and boys tend to have a different approach to working with IT, but it is important to give a more detailed look at the nature of the ways in which children interact with computers and with each other. Observing the complexity of what is happening when children work together around a keyboard will give insight into ways forward in the development of children's attitudes about themselves and each other. There are two broad areas associated with different ways of working: individual learning styles and interaction in groups.

Learning styles Teachers must be aware of the different learning styles which children may adopt in different situations and be careful to provide a range of opportunities and contexts in which they can work. They must also be aware of the need to listen to the children, not only to develop a sensitivity about when and how to intervene, but also to be aware that the interactions between the children are not always what is expected!

An important study in examining assumptions about the ways that girls and boys approach mathematical problem solving was that of Sutherland and Hoyles (Hoyles, 1988). They considered that 'programming' the computer using Logo supported competence and confidence by enabling the pupils to have power or control in the situation. They described previous studies that indicated that girls did not perform as well as boys in programming tasks because of the assumed need for logical and linear planning, a mode which can be alienating to people with different learning styles. However, they highlighted the variety of programming styles that could be used with Logo, which challenged some of these assumptions.

They observed that girls and boys both showed abilities to plan their work, but also demonstrated different approaches to implementing their plans. For example, Sally preferred to test all the elements of her planned program separately in 'direct drive' getting immediate feedback about the working of the elements before linking them as procedures. Asim typed in the 'global plan' and then edited and debugged it as difficulties arose. Both were planning in their own way, and Sutherland and Hoyles emphasized the importance of not assessing children's performance 'in ways that assume a particular approach' (Hoyles, 1988, p. 42). In my own work with children in mixed groups using the Roamer, when plans did not work as expected, the girl in the group suggested trying out 'each little bit first'. She was hushed by the boys who claimed that that would be 'too easy'. (Their solution was to move the obstacle course when they thought I wasn't looking!)

Sherry Turkle also explored different cognitive styles that could be used in programming and in the general operation of IT (Turkle, 1984). She, like Seymour Papert, considers computers to have the potential to be 'objects to think with', and a comfortable relationship with the computer is impor-

111

tant. Many women and men are alienated from new technologies because of the culture of a 'correct' style of interaction – a formal, analytical, 'top-down' approach, which has been seen as traditionally 'male' and 'scientific'. She uses the term 'bricolage' to describe a more flexible style of planning where ideas are developed through brainstorming, association and negotiation, rather than following a formal, linear plan. Turkle and Papert (1990) refer to computers as tools, but raise the possibility of those tools including 'harpsichords' as well as 'hammers'. The increasing use of and confidence with word processors, desktop publishers, art and design packages and hypermedia support this approach to the use of IT, making links and connections between different sources and forms of information.

The implication of this brief discussion of cognitive styles is that teachers providing IT experiences for girls and boys have to consider not only their attitude to the technology, but also the context and demands of the task itself, either in its content, or in the ways in which it can be tackled.

Interaction in groups   There are some intriguing observations of girls and boys working together with IT, in both single-sex and mixed-sex groups. These studies challenge many of the 'common-sense' assumptions made by some teachers about what is going on when the children are 'working on the computer' and indicate that, as Geoffrey Underwood states, 'boys, girls and computers are a dangerous combination' (Underwood, 1994, p. 9).

Many teachers like to mix groups to encourage social interaction and co-operation between girls and boys, but there is much evidence of boys dominating and assuming control whilst girls are literally marginalized. In single-sex groups, girls seem to work more co-operatively, whilst boys work more as individuals, taking turns or giving instructions. Studies of mixed and single-sex groups of young children working together on a language-based task on the computer showed that the mixed groups performed worse than single-sex groups (Underwood and Underwood, 1990). This would seem to point to a case for letting the children work in single-sex groups; but the waters were muddied by a study which indicated that single-sex girls' groups performed less well than mixed groups in a Logo turtle task, suggesting that the girls needed the boys (Hughes *et al.*, 1988).

It was suggested that the spatial rather than linguistic nature of the task in this last study was not as advantageous to girls, and this was echoed in a later problem-solving study where children used an adventure-game format to plan the safe transport of a king's crown, avoiding confrontation with pirates (Barbieri and Light, 1992). Various effects, such as age, cognitive style, social interaction and attitudes, were discussed as factors in the strong performance of the boys and weak performance of the girls without the boys. An interesting twist to the tale, however, was provided by a further study in which the 'king's crown' context was changed to a 'honeybears' one, the problem remaining the same (Littleton *et al.*, 1993). The single-sex girls' groups outperformed the single-sex boys' and mixed groups. It would seem that the girls are much more affected by the context of the problem. An important factor in their performance is the 'level of engagement' with the task as a meaningful and interesting problem, rather than just 'doing it on the computer'. This does indicate that the nature of the task being asked of the children has to be carefully considered, but raises other interesting questions about the differences between girls' and boys' worlds and how they are defined, maintained and valued, by children and by the toy industry's marketing managers.

Another important question, of course, is *why* mixed groups do not work as well with each other. What is the nature of the interaction between children in single-sex and mixed-sex groups which has such an influence on the ways in which they behave and perform?

The key seems to lie in the nature of the *discussion* between the children and the potential that has for understanding of the task and cognitive development. Hoyles (1988) noted that girls worked more co-operatively in groups, helping each other or being prepared to ask for help. When they discussed the value of individual work it was in the way it enabled them to work 'at their own pace'. Boys, however, seemed to have a

113

much more competitive speech style in groups, giving preplanned instructions or commands rather than suggestions for negotiation, and not acknowledging the use of the other people's ideas. They felt that individual work enabled them to get on 'without distraction'.

Geoffrey Underwood and his co-workers designed some studies to look much more closely at the level of the discussion between girls' and boys' single-sex and mixed-sex pairs working with computer-based tasks. They focused on the nature of the discussion between the children in the pairs and the type of group interaction expected, whether collaboration or individual contributions (Underwood *et al.*, 1993, 1994). The most effective style of interaction was full collaboration, where the children made suggestions, considered each other's suggestions, rejected some and accepted others. They were able to resolve 'conflict' between ideas by negotiation and reflection in order to make connections and come to conclusions. This 'group cohesion' was noticed particularly among single-sex pairs of girls' who made contributions which were also evaluative and analytical. The single-sex boys' group also improved their performance when encouraged to collaborate. The mixed groups of girl/boy tended not to perform as well, as their conversation was often quite negative and critical of each other, leading to tension and frustration on both sides.

It is this crucial nature of the discussion in an engaging context which affects the quality of the children's learning. Resolving cognitive conflict through co-operative social interaction can have a powerful influence on thinking skills and is a critical point for teacher intervention, challenge and support (Kruger, 1993). 'The most effective thinkers justify their own ideas and also take account of their partner's suggestions, with the eventual rejection of failed solutions being the best indicator of new understanding' (Underwood, 1994, p. 9).

Culture and class

The effects of gender on IT experience are observed,

discussed and researched in a broad and developing debate. There are, however, other aspects of experience in our society in which access to IT resources can be limited. It can be argued that IT has not brought about the optimistic cultural and cognitive changes predicted and described by writers such as Papert and Turkle, but has reinforced and perpetuated the existing inequalities in gender, culture and socio-economic status in society.

The socio-cultural context has a powerful influence on attitudes to learning, and so it is very likely that cultural factors affect interaction with computers. This is particularly important in relation to language, where the language of the software and general jargon is the second language of the child. Although there are some obvious difficulties in the level of competence in reading and understanding and the degree of support the children are given in working with IT resources, there are some interesting ways in which IT can provide new opportunities for access and participation in the class. Multilingual word processors, such as Allwrite, have been developed to display a wide variety of fonts, scripts and characters – although not translation! Children can therefore have the experience of editing and presenting high-quality printed work in their home language. There are also developments to produce a range of examples of educational software in languages other than English.

Fisher (1993b) reported bilingual pupils working collaboratively with Logo in their own language, producing good-quality work which the teacher could follow in its development to its final form. This also highlighted the shift in role and control for the teacher and increased the confidence of the children. The design of IT resources on CD ROMs, using the facilities for animation, interaction and commentary in different languages, could be very motivating for bilingual children. In one of my own classes, there was a majority of children for whom English was their second language. Logo, word processing and problem-solving packages were popular, and the children were encouraged to take turns as 'monitors' to explain new programs to their friends. This was a particularly significant breakthrough with one boy, Rashid, who gained tremendous confidence by being regarded as 'good at computers' – his first 'success' at school.

There are still concerns about levels of access to information in different socio-economic groups. In the UK the 1991 DES *Survey of Information Technology in Schools* indicated great variation in computer to pupil ratios in primary schools, ranging from 1:211 to 1:5! There were also differences in the capital expenditure on IT resources, which were related to the relative prosperity of the catchment areas of the schools. Eunice Fisher highlighted the differences in funding support for IT equipment from parents in 'relatively prosperous' areas (40 per cent) and 'economically disadvantaged' areas (12 per cent). Prosperous and professional parents are also more likely to have connections to promote sponsorship to supplement IT resources. 'It is difficult to think of any other kind of basic educational resource where such wide variations between the best and the worst equipped schools would be likely to occur' (Fisher, 1993b, p. 77). The presence, power and potential of home computers is broadly related to family income, although ownership is more independent of socio-economic status than is ownership of books. Despite the fact that the minimum equipment to read a CD ROM costs as much as benefit payments to feed a child for 18 months, people do tend to obtain computers, and it will be interesting to see whether recent commercial developments in home computers narrow or widen the gap between the 'haves and have-nots' in terms of access to information and communications.

What can teachers do to ensure IT experiences which promote learning for all children?

Having insight into one's own experiences and attitudes, as well as those of the children in school and at home, will help one to identify and reflect upon one's own beliefs, attitudes and values as these directly affect the ways in which classrooms are organized, learning experiences presented and interactions and interventions encouraged. There are three areas in which issues of equity could be addressed: access to resources, images of IT and the role of the teacher.

ACCESS TO RESOURCES

- Do the tasks asked of the children reflect different cognitive styles and contexts?

- Is there flexibility in the organization of groups to allow for single-sex and mixed-sex groups in different situations?

- Are the children actively encouraged and supported in collaboration and co-operation?

- Is IT capability being developed across the curriculum, to avoid association with particular subjects?

- Is there a relationship between expectations in the classroom and the general equity policy in the school?

- Are the children given the opportunity to relate IT experiences to wider issues of the impact of IT in society?

- Are software and supporting resources selected with the consideration of different interests, languages and ways of working?

IMAGES OF IT

- Has there been thought given to the role models presented by the teachers and IT co-ordinator in terms of gender balance in confidence and expertise?

- Is the expertise of girls and boys recognized throughout the school, or are the IT monitors always year 6 boys?

- Are the children given the opportunity to discuss their images and expectations of themselves and IT, both positive and negative?

THE TEACHER'S ROLE

- Do you take time to listen to the interaction of different groups?

- Do you consider a range of appropriate interventions for social and cognitive interactions?

- Do you challenge bullying, sexism and racism?

- Do you encourage and help to develop collaboration skills?

- Do you encourage 'computer-shy' children to experience a range of activities to help them find a comfortable context?

- Do you attend INSET courses to extend your own confidence and competence with new resources?

There are certainly positive and enabling possibilities for IT in communication and learning, but it is not a neutral technology and its use can reflect influences in society. Access to information is a key to empowerment, but it can be constrained and limited. There are ways to counteract these limitations, which require honest appraisal of experiences and attitudes on the part of teachers, in order to give children opportunities to work and learn in ways which challenge inequity.

CHAPTER 6
Preparation, Planning and Review

When a visitor walks into a classroom with a view to looking at the children's development of IT capability, there are a number of questions to be asked. It does not matter who the visitor is; a student teacher, newly qualified teacher, newly appointed teacher, mentor, tutor, senior teacher or even inspector will all have the same areas of concern, in varying degrees of detail or complexity. These concerns include:

- *Resources.* Which equipment is being used? Which software is being used? How are these organized to allow access for the children?
- *People.* Who manages the organization of IT resources and experiences? Who is the troubleshooter? Who supports whom?
- *Planning and presentation.* How is IT capability planned across the curriculum to provide a good quality of experience for the children which enables continuity and progression? How are these plans organized and implemented on a daily basis? How are the children's experiences recorded and assessed?
- *Quality of IT experience for the children.* What are the children learning about the curriculum area, IT capability and IT in the world at large through the planned activities? How does their work in school relate to their attitude to and experience of IT in the home?
- *Quality of the teachers' experience.* How do the teachers view their role and responsibilities in using IT in the classroom? How does this reflect their own attitude to IT and learning?
- *Practice and policy in the school.* Is there a policy underlying and guiding the work with and management of IT in the whole school? Is there an IT co-ordinator to organize resources and in-service education for the staff?

This chapter will focus on the resources, people and planning from the point of view of a student, newly qualified teacher or teacher lacking confidence or familiarity with IT. It highlights questions which can help in identifying the IT resources available for use in the classroom, the management of resources within the school and the support systems at hand. There are also straightforward suggestions for 'getting going' in order to become familiar with new resources. The process in which the development of IT capability is incorporated into planning across the curriculum will also be outlined and examples given of suggestions for lesson plans.

Resources and people: what to look for in the classroom

It is the interaction and understanding between the people in a school that promote the quality of learning, not the amount and type of equipment provided. It is, however, the equipment which is the easiest to spot and quantify on a first visit to a school, and the following guidelines start with physical resources and move on to the people who use and support them:

- software;
- hardware;
- physical organization;
- support and troubleshooting.

SOFTWARE

Which IT applications are used in the classroom? Is there a basic 'toolkit' of programs appropriate for the age and experience of the children? Which software is used as a word processor, a graphics package, a music program, a data-handling program? Is there an adventure game, a problem-solving activity or a simulation? Is there a version of Logo or a related package? Are there programs specific to a curriculum area such as spelling, number programs, or mapping? Which software is used for control activities?

Are the notes and documentation for the software readily available? It is often difficult if not hopeless to try to use an unfamiliar piece of software without some guidance from published documentation or teacher notes. Never accept a disc without them!

Which pieces of software are used most often in the classroom? It is interesting to see which software available in the classroom is used most often by the children and teachers. A wide range may be available, but only a small number 'tried and tested', either for educational reasons associated with the use in the curriculum, or for technical reasons related to the teacher's familiarity and confidence with particular programs.

How is the software managed? Does each class have a wide range of software available, either on separate disks or stored on the hard disk of the computer, or is there a basic 'toolkit' of software – word processor, graphics, data handling – appropriate for the age of the children? Is the 'toolkit' supplemented by a 'pool' of other titles appropriate for particular topics available to all classes as required? Are the arrangements for the copyright licences for software made clear? (Software companies do not usually allow the copying of their product unless the school has a licence to do so under certain conditions, such as a limited number of copies or restricted use on a specified site. Some local education authorities negotiate licences for all their schools.)

HARDWARE

Teachers and students who are inexperienced with IT in the classroom should take careful note of the type and range of equipment being used, both in the classroom and around the the school.

What type of computers does the school have? In the early 1980s schools tended to use standardized equipment as advised by the local education authority (LEA). This had advantages in the LEA's provision of technical and in-service support for teachers. Many British primary schools have since updated and diversified the types of computer they use, for a variety of reasons, and there are now a large number of possibilities for the types of machine which may be found in the classroom.

It is at this point that the eyes of many people not interested in the technical details of IT begin to glaze over. It is important, however, to know which *type* and *model* of micro is being used, as the power and the memory capacity of the computer might affect the software applications that can be run. An analogy could be drawn with the expectations one could have of the speed and performance of a Morris Minor and a Mercedes.

Commonly found models of computer are RM (Nimbus or PC models), Acorn (Archimedes, A series or RISC/PC), Apple Macintosh or IBM PC or 'clones' (a wide range of models), Acorn BBC or BBC Master, Amstrad and Atari. Although the type of computer will determine the software which can be used with it, new developments in hardware are moving towards 'transparency', in that all types of software will soon be recognized by different manufacturers' machines. The Acorn RISC/PC and the Apple PowerMac provide the capability of running software for the PC as well as their own software, Acorn or Macintosh. The new micros currently being produced are 'multimedia' computers, that is they combine text, visual images and sound in the applications, can use information stored on CD ROM, and can also be linked to communications networks.

What variety of computers is there? Although most classrooms will have a 'desktop' computer, some will also have portable computers such as laptops, notebooks and palmtops available for the children. These could be dedicated to particular tasks such as word processing or datalogging, or available to be carried around and taken on field trips. Data saved on the portable machines can be transferred to desktop machines for development work on a larger screen or to use fixed printing facilities.

Are there printers available with the micros? Each micro should have access to a printer, either dedicated to a particular machine or shared between several machines on a network.

There are many different types of printer, the simplest and cheapest at the moment being black and white 'dot matrix' printers, which give a 'dotty' effect to the printed characters. More expensive but higher-quality printers are now being used in schools, from bubble-jet and colour printers to laser printers.

Do the computers use a WIMPs environment? Most micros now use a graphical system or 'interface' in which the user moves a 'mouse pointer' to select and manipulate icons or pictures on the screen to operate software applications. WIMPs stands for 'windows, icons, menus and pointers', which appear on the screen as tools to organize the tasks, the metaphor being that of a desk top on which files, documents and tools can be moved around, opened, closed or thrown away. Microsoft (used on PC computers), Apple Macintosh and Acorn window environments are similar in the principles of operation, although there are some distinct differences which need to be practised. Older machines, such as the RML 480Z or Acorn BBC, do not use a windows environment, and the user gives direct commands to the computer from the keyboard, either by typing in words or by pressing combinations of keys, such as the SHIFT and BREAK keys to start up a piece of software.

How are the micros made accessible to the children? Many primary schools use 'stand-alone' computers, which are independent and usually have their own software and printer. Some, however, use 'networks' of computers, where the micros are linked together by cables, often across distances between rooms throughout the building, in order to share software and printing facilities.

Do the computers have hard disks and/or floppy disks? Floppy disks can store the programs to be used, such as a word processor or graphics package, and the documents or files created by the user. These are then placed in the disk drive in order to load the software into the 'workspace' of the computer as required. The amount of memory, measured in 'megabytes' or 'mb' available for the 'workspace' will affect the speed and number of the applications running at a time. That is, a machine with 8 mb will operate faster than one with 2 mb.

A hard disk, however, is memory for storage in the computer itself and provides the capacity for many applications and files at once, rather like an internal box of floppy disks. It is therefore efficient to have all the software available for loading from the hard disc and use the separate floppy disks to store or back up individual children's work, whether it be a written document, database or electronic painting.

Does the computer use CD ROMs? More computers are now linked to or fitted with a CD ROM drive which will read information from CD ROMs, just as it would from any other disc. It is not yet possible, however, to save children's work on to a CD ROM. CD ROMs have a large capacity and can store data as text, sound and visual images, still and moving, and they provide access to multimedia information. Some schools may have interactive video systems, in which a large video disc provides the text, images and sound, controlled by either a computer, hand set or bar-code reader.

Are there concept keyboards available? Concept keyboards provide an alternative means of communicating with the computer to the QWERTY keyboard. This can be very useful with children of all ages who do not have the motor co-ordination – or patience – to type in text character by character. A concept keyboard is a flat board, usually A4 or A3 size, which is attached to the computer by a cable. A paper overlay, prepared by the teacher or distributed with specific software, is placed on the board. This can be designed to show pictures, words, sentences, numbers and sequences. The computer can be programmed to recognize when certain areas of the overlay have been pressed by the children in order to give a certain response, from showing a corresponding picture or word on the screen to moving through an adventure game.

Are there any programmable toys or turtles? Devices such as Roamers, Pips or turtle robots, which are attached directly to the computer and controlled by commands, can all be used in investigations with IT. Direct commands or sequences can be given to instruct them to move around in physical space.

Is there equipment for sensing, measurement and control? Controlling and monitoring external events requires extra equipment to be linked to the computer to process and display information. Input and output devices such as pressure sensors and motors are connected to the micro through a 'buffer box'. These boxes can sometimes log data independently of the computer, for example on field trips or over a long period of time, and then be linked later to represent the collected data as graphs on the computer screen or print out the information in a variety of forms.

Are there any other devices for input of information? Scanners, digitizers, microphones and digital cameras can all be used to convert information from the world outside into digital form for use and manipulation by appropriate software, such as a graphics package for visual images or a music package for sound.

Is there other specialist equipment available? It is useful to find out whether there is a specialist or enthusiast in the school who has been able to develop IT in a particular area, such as music or photography. It is also interesting to ask which resources people would like to have available in their classrooms!

PHYSICAL ORGANIZATION

How are the IT resources made available? Are the computers in the classroom or in a separate resource area? Are they in a room set aside for computers? How many computers are available for the class? Are there any 'pooled' computers that can be brought into classrooms if extra are required? Are there laptops or other portables available? Are the concept keyboards, Roamers, Pips and other resources kept in the classroom or in a central 'pool'?

How is the classroom space organized for the use of IT? Are the computers on trolleys? Is there space for other work resources such as paper, books or maths equipment? Is there space for the children to sit in pairs or threes and have room to discuss what they are doing as well as take turns in using the keyboard? Where do the children go to work with Roamers and programmable toys?

How are the support materials made available for the children? Are the disks, help cards and notes clearly labelled and easily accessible to the children? Can the children select and load the right software for the task; that is, do they know the purpose of the different programs available? Have the children written their own help cards to assist each other?

Are Health and Safety issues considered? Are Health and Safety issues taken into account in terms of the safety of the electrical sockets, leads and connections, the clarity and position of the screen, and the seating arrangements? LEAs and advisory teams will inform the school of the latest regulations for health and safety.

SUPPORT AND TROUBLESHOOTING

Who is the first person to call? Is there an IT co-ordinator in the school with technical and educational expertise to support staff? Who is responsible for managing the software and hardware resources? Who is the first person to call if there are any difficulties? Is this a teacher or a child?

Is support provided outside the school? Are there links with an advisory service or professional centre for technical and educational support? Are there links with parents for classroom support, technical advice or fund raising?

Getting started with IT resources

STARTING OUT

Becoming familiar with the IT resources, hardware and software does take *time*, as it would with any other new resource in the classroom. Teachers would not dream of introducing a new maths scheme or reading a book to the children without previous preparation. It cannot be assumed that IT can be used effectively in the classroom by just switching on the computer, loading a program and leaving the children to get on with it.

It is therefore very important that teachers and students who are unfamiliar or not confident with a particular piece of software or new equipment should spend some time exploring the resources. Documentation and notes are notoriously obscure to the novice, and it is always helpful to have a colleague or child who does know the system available to answer questions. Many people find that they learn their IT skills in a haphazard fashion by asking friends and colleagues about particular features or problems in a context, rather than working through a manual or watching a demonstration. As teachers we should be sensitive to different learning styles both for ourselves and for others, and therefore allow time for exploration, uncertainty and lack of confidence; creating an atmosphere in which the learners are not afraid to admit to difficulties or ask questions.

Unfortunately there are occasions when the world of IT is seen as an opportunity for one-upmanship, demonstration of technical expertise and knowledge of the latest developments. IT is not effectively used in the classroom, however, unless the teacher has an understanding of the educational purpose of the activity in the first place. The presence of IT resources in the classroom does not take away the established expertise, experience and educational judgement of the teacher.

When encountering new resources, it is useful to ask a colleague or child to be available for questions during a 'hands-on' session. Some people prefer to see resources demonstrated first, others prefer to have a go and then ask why certain things happen as they do. The following steps are an absolute beginner's guide to getting started and having a go:

1 Find out if there are any help cards or notes available. Some people find it useful to make notes as they go along with a new activity.
2 Check that everything is switched on.
3 Ask whether the system is set up ready to save and print out work. Some computers are set up as soon as they are switched on, others may need to have 'printer drivers'

and extras loaded. The IT co-ordinator should be aware of the set-up of the classroom system.

4 Find out whether children's or teachers' work is saved on to a separate floppy disk, and have one ready if necessary.

5 If the working environment of the computer is unfamiliar, practise the operation of the mouse and pointer, clicking and dragging to open, close and move windows and menus.

6 Locate the software on the hard disk, floppy disk or CD ROM and the accompanying notes.

7 Load the software by the procedures appropriate to the type of computer. A windows environment will probably require the opening of directory windows and folders, and the selecting and loading of software by clicking on icons representing the required application.

8 Work through some of the features of the software, but do not feel that the whole program needs to be seen at the first sitting.

9 Save the work, such as the written text, picture, database or position in an adventure game. Different systems and programs may have slightly different methods for saving work, so it is important to check the procedures the first time to ensure that the work is saved in the right place.

10 Print out any work to practise the procedures, from setting up the paper in the printer, through sending the document or picture, to leaving the printer in a suitable state for the next user.

11 Close down the program and the system 'neatly' to ensure that everything is saved and finished off, either ready for use by the next person or shut down completely.

12 Remove the floppy disks or CD ROMs and switch everything off.

There are many introductory guides and tutorials available for the different types of micro and the software. LEA advisory teams often provide HelpCards and support for those unfamiliar with fast-changing systems.

There have been many schemes, guidelines and checklists produced to help teachers evaluate software for use in the classroom, the most valuable dealing with ways to observe the ways in which children use the resources (Wellington, 1985; Blease, 1986). There follows a set of questions which help to focus on three areas when considering these pieces of software:

1 the design and appropriate use of the software;
2 the appropriate use of the resources with particular children or in a particular context;
3 the different teaching styles and models of classroom management that could be developed in using these pieces of software.

The design and appropriate use of the software

- Is the program easy to load, operate and finish?
- Are the notes clear and efficient?
- Is the design of the software clear? Consider the graphics, screen presentation, sound, controlling keys or mouse actions, routes through the program, use of menus and instructions, speed of presentation, etc.
- Was the program clearly organized for teacher and pupil use? Was there a facility for the teacher to set up the activity in a particular way?

The appropriate use of the resources with particular children or in a particular context

- Does the program deal with a particular content area or concept?
- Does it enhance or extend existing resources in this area or would it replace a perfectly good method that you already use?
- Is the program motivating and engaging for the children?
- Was the language level of any text used on the screen appropriate for the target users?

- How was a wrong response dealt with?
- Were the children's responses recorded in any way for the teacher to see?
- Is the program specific in its aims and purpose and clear in providing feedback to the user?
- Is the program open-ended, enabling the users to adapt and develop their activity?
- What do the children think of the program? What do they think it is for, and do they enjoy using it?

The different teaching styles and models of classroom management that could be developed in using these pieces of software

- Is the program designed for a particular teaching style or method?
- Can the activity be introduced and sustained in a variety of ways, such as teacher demonstration, cascade instruction, collaboration within a group, individual work, one-off session, several sessions, etc?
- Does the teacher need to prepare or collect supporting resources for the activity, and how could the resources be incorporated into the 'normal' classroom organization?

Planning IT capability

Having become more familiar with the technical aspects of the resources, and having thought about their suitability for use by children, it is essential that children's experience of IT and development of IT capability is planned across the curriculum. As defined in the National Curriculum, IT capability is:

characterised by an ability to use effectively IT tools and information sources to analyse, process and present information, and to model, measure and control external events. This involves:

- using information sources and IT tools to solve problems
- using IT tools and information sources, such as computer systems and software packages, to support learning in a variety of contexts
- understanding the implications of IT for working life and society

Pupils should be given opportunities, where appropriate, to develop and apply their IT capability in their study of National Curriculum subjects.

(DfE, 1995, p. 1)

This IT capability is not a subject in its own right but developed through use in other areas of the curriculum, providing insight into the nature of the different subjects and integration between distinctive subject domains. The Dearing Report highlighted this approach in Key Stages 1 and 2: 'The knowledge, understanding and skills of information technology should be ... taught through all relevant curriculum subjects at both key stages' (Dearing, 1994, 4.21). Planning the development of IT capability for the children should therefore be embedded in the curriculum planning in the school. Continuity and progression in IT capability can be mapped on to the children's developing experience of the curriculum throughout their school career.

Many schools set up procedures for planning, recording and assessment through discussion with the staff, and frameworks are designed which reflect different strengths and ways of working to provide the whole, basic and national curriculum for the children. Long-term planning will provide continuity and progression by identifying broad themes, topics or a subject focus for each year group. These can be broken down into more detail for termly, half-termly or fortnightly plans, from which teachers will plan their weekly and daily activities, perhaps working with other teachers in the year group and pooling resources.

The Programmes of Study for IT capability in KS1 and KS2 have therefore to be interpreted both in terms of the ways in which they can be presented through the curriculum subjects and in terms of the resources which might be available and appropriate for the children in particular years. Many schools outline the expectations for each year group in each area of the curriculum, including IT, and then use those outlines to map out the connections between the curriculum areas within a topic or theme for each of those year groups. Such a mapping exercise enables the staff to consider the balance and

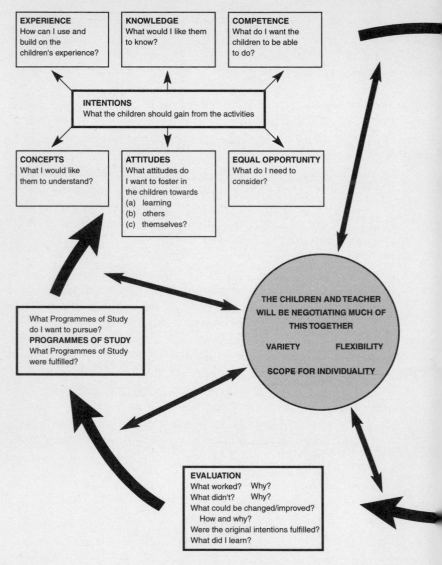

Figure 6.1 An aid to primary curriculum planning.
Source: North London Language Consortium, reproduced with permission.

CURRICULUM PLANNING

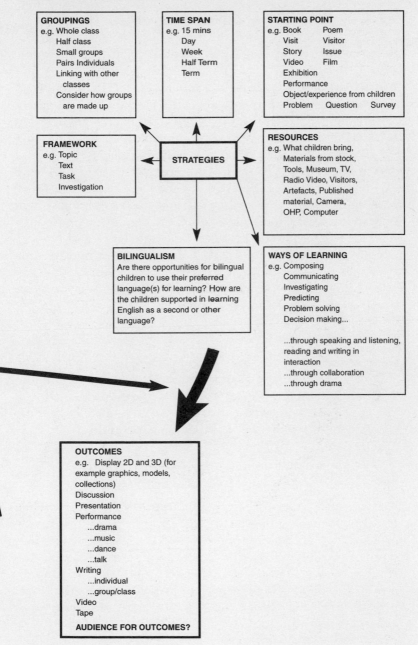

GROUPINGS
e.g. Whole class
Half class
Small groups
Pairs Individuals
Linking with other
classes
Consider how groups
are made up

TIME SPAN
e.g. 15 mins
Day
Week
Half Term
Term

STARTING POINT
e.g. Book   Poem
Visit   Visitor
Story   Issue
Video   Film
Exhibition
Performance
Object/experience from children
Problem   Question   Survey

FRAMEWORK
e.g. Topic
Text
Task
Investigation

STRATEGIES

RESOURCES
e.g. What children bring,
Materials from stock,
Tools, Museum, TV,
Radio Video, Visitors,
Artefacts, Published
material, Camera,
OHP, Computer

BILINGUALISM
Are there opportunities for bilingual
children to use their preferred
language(s) for learning? How are
the children supported in learning
English as a second or other
language?

WAYS OF LEARNING
e.g. Composing
Communicating
Investigating
Predicting
Problem solving
Decision making...

...through speaking and listening,
reading and writing in
interaction
...through collaboration
...through drama

OUTCOMES
e.g.   Display 2D and 3D (for
example graphics, models,
collections)
Discussion
Presentation
Performance
...drama
...music
...dance
...talk
Writing
...individual
...group/class
Video
Tape

AUDIENCE FOR OUTCOMES?

continuity within the curriculum in the children's experience.

A useful framework for planning and assessment throughout these stages, from a long-term curriculum map to a specific session plan, is the North London Language Consortium's 'Aid to Primary Planning' (Figure 6.1). This framework emphasizes the cyclical nature of planning, teaching and learning, and evaluation, and recognizes that assessment lies at the heart of the process of promoting children's learning, providing both 'feedback' and 'feedforward' to teachers.

Such an approach focuses on the programmes of study and learning intentions underlying themes and activities, rather than on 'topic titles'. Learning intentions are defined as 'what we want the children to know, understand and be able to do' – the experience, knowledge, concepts, attitudes and competences that could be developed. This enables teachers to identify areas which can be addressed by a cross-curricular approach, and those which may need a specific subject focus. It also encourages clarity in approaching the development of IT capability in that:

- the focus on learning intentions provides some coherence in the children's experience of the subject areas and indicates the purpose and context for using IT;
- the IT skills required to support the learning can be identified along with other skills and competences.

IT capability is therefore embedded in the curriculum planning, not a 'bolt-on' extra.

Having stated the learning intentions for the children, the strategies for presenting and organizing activities to support this learning can be developed. It is then possible to see how to provide a range of IT experiences for all the children in the class over a period of time. Not every child would have to do the same activity 'on the computer'; they could meet the learning intentions for IT capability in a variety of contexts. Planning these strategies should then lead to a range of outcomes and a clear view of the audience for the 'end result', whether it be a display, discussion or presentation.

Two examples of the ways in which IT capability can be incorporated into such planning are given in Figures 6.2–6.5.

The first is based upon work carried out in a year 2 class, illustrating a medium-term plan (Figure 6.2) and a session plan (Figure 6.3) for an activity which focuses on history, supported by English, art and IT capability. The session plan highlights the use of IT in art. The second is based upon work carried out in a year 6 class, focusing on design and technology, English, maths, science and IT capability (Figure 6.4). The session plan (Figure 6.5) highlights an activity with control technology. The appropriate Programmes of Study (PoS) for IT capability have been stated, although the PoS for each subject area would also be available to the teachers in the planning process. The two plans indicate different approaches to identifying learning intentions, the first stating overall concepts, knowledge and skills, the second retaining the subject headings.

The assessment of the children's learning and evaluation for future planning should be clearly related to the initial learning intentions, and evidence sought through various strategies such as observations, discussions, final 'products' and presentations. Children can be involved in the recording of progression of their IT capability across the curriculum. Some schools use recording sheets attached to pieces of work in conjunction with summary sheets, which indicate different activities and degrees of support the child has experienced. The children could record given statements such as:

	I had some help	I did it in a group	I had no help	I helped others
I worked with a computer.				
I saved my work and loaded it back later.				
I used a computer to draw a picture.				

Or they could write in their own activities, which the teacher could then match to the general learning intentions and level descriptions for IT capability:

	I had some help	I did it in a group	I had no help	I helped others
I wrote an article for the class newspaper.				
It took me two days to edit and publish it.				
I put the writing and illustrations together using Pendown.				
I collected information about the minibeasts using the CD ROM and making my own database with Junior Pinpoint.				
I presented my results by using graphs and writing a report for the class assembly using Pendown.				

Planning and assessment should both be addressed within the school curriculum framework, clearly indicating the purpose for IT capability, developing within the curriculum context for the children.

Reviewing IT

The previous three sections have outlined the process that students and teachers need to go through, from becoming familiar with IT resources to assessing the level of children's IT capability, in order to support the children's learning.

Evaluating the quality of the children's experience is important in the school, not only to meet the criteria of visiting Office for Standards in Education (OFSTED) inspectors, but also to improve and develop in the long term.

The Framework for the Inspection of Schools (OFSTED, 1994) highlights two key areas for reporting in an inspection:

1   standards of achievement;
2   quality of learning.

It also identifies nine essential factors which contribute to these areas:

1   quality of teaching;
2   assessment, recording and reporting;
3   quality and range of the curriculum;
4   equality of opportunity;
5   provision for pupils with special educational needs;
6   management and administration;
7   teaching and non-teaching staff;
8   resources and learning;
9   accommodation.

The NCET has published *Reviewing IT,* a useful set of materials to assist schools in preparing for inspections and monitoring the development of IT capability (NCET, 1994e). These highlight the key areas and contributing factors, describing the evaluation criteria for inspection in good and unsatisfactory situations. It is interesting to note the indicators which are suggested for the factor of 'quality of teaching':

Where teaching with or about IT is good, the following statements are likely to be true:

1   Individual lesson planning takes account of the school's agreed approach to the development of IT capability
2   Lesson objectives identify specific gains in IT capability, where appropriate
3   Teachers take pupils' prior experience with IT (gained in and out of school) into account when planning lessons
4   Lessons exhibit adequate differentiation such that tasks set match the needs and abilities of pupils
5   Teachers successfully exploit the power of IT to motivate learning and to sustain pupils' interest
6   IT is used to enhance both teaching and learning in a range of subject contexts
7   Teachers adopt classroom management strategies which reflect the availability and use of IT resources
8   Teachers with a restricted experience of IT do not allow this to limit the opportunities that they provide to pupils
9   Teachers exploit those occasions when some pupils have IT skills which they, themselves, have not yet acquired
10 Available support (internal or external to the school) such as technicians, teachers with an IT specialism or SEN specialists is used by the teachers to the best effect.

(NCET, 1994e, p. 5)

137

Concepts

What do we want the children to understand?
- understanding sequence of events in a story about the past
- empathy for people's actions in past events; being able to suggest reasons for their actions
- understanding that a past event can be interpreted differently depending on who recounts the event and who is listening
- understanding differences between past and present times
- understanding ideas, methods and approaches used in different styles and traditions

Competences

What do we want the children to do?
- sequence events
- write collaboratively
- draft, edit, publish
- generate text and pictures, save, retrieve, edit and print
- communicate meaning for a chosen audience
- choose an appropriate format for presentation with IT
- retell a story from a different perspective
- experiment with tools for drawing and painting
- experiment with visual elements to make images

Knowledge

What do we want the children to know?
Certain conventions (when editing) help the reader to understand the writing

Equal Opportunities

Awareness of certain children in groups, particularly boys and girls in IT groups

Time span

Over one week with other activites

Experience

How can we use and build on the children's past experience?

Starting Point

Listen to the story

Framework

- whole class listen to story
- divide story into sections
- look at and discuss picture of Bayeaux tapestry
- working in pairs – write own section/paint illustrations
- discussion of end product – how different would it be if told from a different point of view?

Ways of Learning

- collaboration
- communication
- through talk
- through writing
- through listening

Resources

- The teacher!
- paper, paint, collage materials
- picture of Bayeaux tapestry
- A4000 computer
- WP ..Phases 3
- Graphics ..Easel 3
- tape recorder
- video

Outcomes/Audiences

Story retold in sections with illustrations like the tapestry.. wall display and class book of writing and painting.... tapes of children's stories....
Alternative versions told and presented

Opportunities for Assessment

- spontaneous observations
- planned observations during activities
- discussions with the children during and after activity
- looking at writing, paintings, word processing and graphics images

Programmes of Study

IT capability
2a generate and communicate their ideas in different forms, using text.... pictures and sound
1c examine and discuss their experiences of IT, and look at the uses of IT in the outside world

Intentions

Strategies

Outcomes and Audience

The legend of Anne Frieda

Evaluation

Programmes of Study

Figure 6.2 A planning frame for a Year 2 class (developed from material first produced by Jane Treacher for East Sussex LEA and reproduced with permission).

138

Competences
What do we want the children to do?
- generate pictures with IT, save, retrieve, edit and print
- experiment with tools and techniques for painting images
- experiment with visual elements to make images

Programmes of Study... Art
Investigating and Making
- review and modify what they have done and describe what they might change or develop in future work

Knowledge and Understanding
- recognize visual elements in images
- describe works of art... in simple terms and explain what they think and feel about these

Programmes of Study... IT capability
1c examine and discuss their experiences of IT, and look at the uses of IT in the outside world
2a generate and communicate their ideas in different forms, using... pictures

Opportunities for Assessment
- spontaneous observations
- planned observations during activities
- discussions with the children during and after activity
- looking at paintings and print outs

Equal Opportunities
Awareness of certain children in groups, particularly boys and girls in the pairs

Time span
Over two afternoons with each group

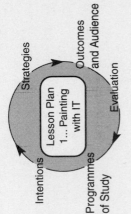

Strategies

Intentions

Outcomes and Audience

Evaluation

Programmes of Study

Lesson Plan 1... Painting with IT

Resources
- painting from previous day
- A4000 computer and printer, discs for saving work
- graphics.. Easel 3

Outcomes/Audiences
Wall display and class book of colour print outs and paintings

Experience
Check which children have already used the graphics package

Activity
- With whole of Green Group (8 children) Discuss the ideas behind the children's paintings from yesterday – ideas for telling the story, paints and colours used, techniques used, advantages and disadvantages, alternative ways of producing an illustration etc
- With first pair...
  Demonstrate the graphics program – mouse movements and buttons, brush, spray and fill tools, colour palette
- Subsequent pairs demonstrate to each other
- Children experiment with different tools, colours and sizes. Save work and print out.
- Discuss ways to use the tools and develop the ideas to illustrate the story and add to the ideas in the paintings... e.g. figures or patterns, colours, effects of tools etc
- Develop work from previous explorations. Save and print out
- Compare first and second attempts and discuss differences between each other and with the painting

Figure 6.3 An activity plan for a Year 2 class (developed from material first produced by Jane Treacher for East Sussex LEA and reproduced with permission).

139

D&T
- generate, develop and evaluate a design
- select materials, make, evaluate and improve the product
- develop understanding of materials, structures, control quality and health and safety

Language
- use talk to investigate, predict and hypothesise, to plan, to present more demanding information in ways helpful to the listener
- listen to others and respect other speakers' contributions
- write report collaboratively
- use writing to communicate ideas and results
- redraft, edit, publish using an appropriate format

IT capability
- use IT to communicate information using text and visual images
- devise a set of instructions to monitor and control a working model

Science
- simple circuits

Maths
- understanding and using measures

Programmes of Study

IT capability
1a use IT to explore and solve problems in the context of work across a variety of subjects
1c discuss their experiences of using IT and assess its value in their working practices
1d investigate parallels with the use of IT in the wider world
2a use IT equipment and software to communicate ideas and information in different forms, incorporating text, graphs, pictures and sound, as appropriate, showing sensitivity to the needs of the audience
3a create, test, modify and store sequences of instructions to control events
3b use IT equipment and software to monitor external events

Equal Opportunities
awareness of certain children in groups, particularly boys and girls in IT groups

Time span
Over three weeks with other activities... Control sessions timetabled

Experience
How can we use and build on the children's past experience?

Framework
- whole class given Exhibition entry challenge
- groups of 4
- direct teaching session of joining and use of equipment and simple circuits
- working in groups – design and make model house shell
- group demonstrations of control technology equipment... software, sensors and outputs
- groups to write procedures e.g.sensing intruders, switching on lights and remote opening of doors

Ways of Learning
- collaboration, • communication
- through talk, • through listening
- through planning and evaluation

Resources
- entry forms and design brief
- materials and tools
- A4000 computer
- WP. Pendown
- graphics.. Revelation
- control technology.. CoCo kit
- display area

Outcomes/Audiences
- exhibition of security systems... working models, presentation posters and leaflets
- diaries kept of process

Starting Point
Applications for 'House Security Systems' Exhibitions. Briefs given

Opportunities for Assessment
- spontaneous observations
- planned observations during activities
- discussions with the children during and after activity
- looking at presentations, models and diaries

Strategies

Intentions

Outcomes and Audience

Evaluation

House Security Exhibition

Programmes of Study

Figure 6.4 A planning frame for a Year 6 class (developed from material first produced by Jane Treacher for East Sussex LEA and reproduced with permission).

Activity
- demonstrate Coco kit to first group of 4... interface, outputs, sensors
- allow time for exploration and play with the kit
- discuss commands Switch on, Wait, Repeat and relate to building procedures in Logo
- allow time to play
- discuss the problem of switching on the lights in the house and the motor for the garage door.
- children to devise procedure for timed lights
- discuss sensors and commands to monitor input
- children to devise procedures to link input and output
- discuss and modify results
- link up sensors and outputs to model houses

Time span
Over three weeks with other activities... Control sessions timetabled... 2 afternoons for each group of 4?

Ways of Learning
- collaboration, • communication
- through talk, • through listening
- through planning and evaluation

Resources
- model houses
- A4000 computer
- control technology... CoCo kit (6 sets of sensors, bulbs, buzzers and motors)

Equal Opportunities
Awareness of certain children in groups, particularly boys and girls in IT groups

Previous experience
Discuss Logo commands and procedures

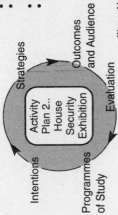

Intentions

Strategies

Outcomes and Audience

Evaluation

Programmes of Study

Activity Plan 2... House Security Exhibition

IT capability
- devise a set of instructions to monitor and control a working model
- investigate parallels with the use of IT in the wider world, consider the effects of such uses and compare them with other methods

Language
- use talk to investigate, predict and hypothesise, to plan, to present more demanding information in ways helpful to the listener
- listen to others and respect other speakers' contributions

Opportunities for Assessment
- spontaneous observations
- planned observations during activities
- discussions with the children during and after activity
- looking at procedures and working models

Outcomes/Audiences
- procedures for switching lights and motors
- working model of house with security system

Figure 6.5 An activity frame for a Year 6 class (developed from material first produced by Jane Treacher for East Sussex LEA and reproduced with permission).

This is indeed a challenging description of good practice, but relates directly to the issues raised in this chapter. In order to develop good-quality teaching with IT, students and teachers need to be familiar with the learning environment in which they are working: the resources, the people, the policies and the curriculum planning. This may involve overcoming anxieties and lack of confidence with a new area, and the commitment of time, but this will be richly compensated when the children do begin to develop their IT capability, making connections between skills and their appropriate application, enriching and enhancing their learning across the curriculum.

CHAPTER 7
The Role of IT in the Primary Classroom

What is the role of IT in the primary classroom? What part can IT play in the teaching and learning which is our central concern? What are the contributions it might make to learning, the challenges it makes to ways of working and the constraints and disadvantages it may bring?

New technologies can widen the variety of places for learning from beyond the classroom to include the back bedroom, the board room or the Byte Café. They provide access to the retrieval and manipulation of information and networks of communication. The 'information society' collects, selects and presents information both to capture and to divert attention, and children are demonstrating 'emergent capabilities' as information handlers in a society which teachers need to understand and relate to teaching and learning (Heppell, 1994). Such changes in the development and impact of IT call for a wider definition of 'literacy' – the three Rs demanded of an educated person in the nineteenth century have been extended in the twentieth to include an understanding and competence in many more areas of experience (Beynon and Mackay, 1993).

New technologies also widen the definitions of the roles of teachers and learners and raise new challenges for teachers in their understanding and use of IT to support learning. *The ImpacT Report* was a large-scale study commissioned by the Department for Education to evaluate the impact of IT on children's achievements in primary and secondary schools (Watson, 1993, p. 4). This research highlighted the finding that in 'particular circumstances IT had a highly positive impact'. The relationships between the 'particular circumstances' were complex and included a number of elements such as access to resources, the nature of those resources and the ways in which pupils could work with them. Important factors were the individual teachers' skills, understanding and initiative in the philosophical underpinning of their work, the organization and management of their IT resources, and the choice of appropriate teaching styles.

I have argued that the use of IT does make a contribution to learning in that it can support the curriculum and provide a variety of ways of working with and approaching problems; that it can be a tool, a resource and a catalyst for thought. I have also argued that teachers need to have an IT capability themselves, an awareness of the advantages and disadvantages of using IT, and an understanding of the wider context in which the children are working. There is a need for teachers to have a confident and informed vision of the future: learning environments which use new technologies will look very different from the schools and classrooms of today, despite resistance to change over the past hundred and twenty years! (Papert commented (1993) that, unlike a surgeon from the past, a time-travelling teacher from the last century would not find much changed in the general classroom technologies used.)

Previous chapters have considered the ways in which IT can make a contribution to learning in the curriculum in communicating and handling information, modelling, monitoring and controlling through different paradigms for learning: instructional, revelatory, conjectural and emancipatory. The use of IT in this way has been set against the backdrop of its potential to empower or constrain children's abilities and expectations and the ways in which teachers need to consider the planning and organization of IT resources in the classroom. This chapter will attempt to round off the discussion of the 'role of IT' by looking more closely at the classroom experience for children, teachers and students, and then broadening the view to consider current developments which may point the way to the future.

The children's experience

Whilst considering the details of resource management, planning, preparation and assessment, it is essential not to lose sight of the quality of the children's experience of IT, both in their development of IT capability and in their understanding of different areas of the curriculum. Their experience encompasses their attitudes to IT in their work in school, their use of IT at home and their understanding of their own achievements. They can develop confidence by using IT in particular situations, by working through difficulties and frustrations with the technology, and by being involved in the evaluation and assessment of their work. They can also undergo different ways of working and learning as individuals and in groups and have distinctive experiences of being girls and boys working with new technology. It is important for teachers to give the children the opportunity to discuss these elements in order to be aware of and reflect upon the attitudes and approaches to work that the children develop in the classroom.

ATTITUDES TO IT

What are the children's ideas and feelings about using IT in their work? Do they see activities using a computer as more interesting than other methods, or do they view them as dull and slow compared to games played at home? Which activities are viewed as more popular than others? Which are considered to be more 'play' than 'work'? Does having a computer at home make a difference to work with IT in school? Do the children understand how IT supports their classroom work and what might be the point of using it in certain situations?

Teachers need to be aware of the children's understanding not only of the place and potential of IT in their daily lives, but also of the purpose of using it in their curriculum work. Knowing the reason for using IT for a certain task will help them to select the appropriate IT tool for other situations. Being able to talk about their feelings and attitudes to IT will also help them to identify the positive aspects which they find engaging and the negative points which cause frustration or anxiety. The excitement of playing an adventure game or developing a class newspaper can be deflated so easily by clumsiness using the keyboard, a faulty disk or a missing printer driver.

APPROACHES TO WORKING WITH IT

Confidence and autonomy   When working with IT, are the children autonomous in choosing the resources, or are they directed? Are they able to set up and operate software with confidence in order to fulfil their task? It is useful to set up systems for assistance and the passing on of tips and hints between the children, teacher and classroom helpers. Clearly labelled disks, notes and help cards are valuable resources. Children can set up a 'chain' of expertise, one child demonstrating a new application and monitoring another child, who then supports another. Some classes have a routine at the beginning of the year to award a 'certificate' to children who can set up a program and teach a friend, the certificate being loaded in a word processor, amended to show the child's name, printed out and then saved for the next child – direct evidence of competence!

Are the children involved in recording and evaluating their IT experiences? An understanding of their own achievement and the ways of showing evidence of a process and a product will help the children build up a sense of their own progression, strengths and areas for further development. They can also be involved in evaluating different pieces of software from a child's point of view, considering the usefulness in the task, ease of use, level of interest and design, and making suggestions for improvements.

Collaborative learning with IT   In addition to thinking about the children's work and attitudes as individuals, the contribution that IT can make to collaborative learning and group work should be considered seriously. Asking the children to work in pairs or groups with the computer is not necessarily just related to the limited IT resources often found in primary classrooms! There are many sound educational reasons for group work, from cognitive and social development of the children to the flexibility in organization for the teacher. The importance of group work in the development of co-operative and collaborative learning has been recognized by many commentators and researchers, from the Plowden Report to the National Curriculum (Bennett and Dunne, 1992; Dean, 1992; Galton and Williamson, 1992; Moyles, 1992; Pollard and Tann, 1993). Children can be organized in groups for different reasons according to different criteria, such as interest, ability and friendship, but it is important to be aware of the nature of the children's learning experiences in those group activities. There is a great difference between genuine co-operation and the convenience of seating children together to work in parallel as individuals.

A study in the United States looked at the possibilities of organizing three groups doing similar activities with different expectations of the groups. Some were 'co-operative', and told that their assessment would be an average of the group's scores; some 'competitive', where the scores were given in relation to the relative performance in the group; and some 'individual', and told that their scores were related to an external standard (Johnson *et al.*, 1986). The group working co-operatively showed significantly higher levels of achievement and demonstrated a way of working which was more independent of the teacher and more open to each other in the group.

The ability to co-operate, discuss and negotiate with others, and function in a team is a key quality in most areas of work, whether as a scientist or as a musician. Each participant of the group brings his or her own experience and background to a situation, and 'two heads are better than one' where it is useful to try out ideas and develop suggestions and starting points. Groups of children working together, either in a group around a computer or as individuals working with a micro on each desk, use each other for tips, hints and suggestions. Sheingold and the group of research workers in Bank Street College described ways of working as including 'dropping in', asking for help from experts and collaboration (Sheingold *et al.*, 1984). Underwood and Underwood (1990) also noted the advantages of the children teaching each other in the development of a more evaluative and reflective approach to forming questions.

The opportunity to talk through one's ideas and consider other people's in order to arrive at a group solution is one of the most powerful aspects of collaborative work. Hoyles *et al.*, (1990) referred to this process as *distancing*, in that one's thoughts are articulated and become the objects of reflection and modification. This is particularly important when perceptions of what is going on and what should happen are different within the group and the conflict and mismatch has to be

147

resolved. Observations of children working together with Logo demonstrated that the children were involved as much with high-level group discussion and problem solving as with individual discovery (Hughes, 1990). There is also anecdotal evidence of the quality of children's talk and concentration as a group involved in collaborative writing around a screen, as changes to words and phrases can be made easily and clearly seen and 'owned' by the whole group.

Curiously, IT has the potential to promote real collaboration in group learning, from discussion around an adventure game to collaborative writing, in ways that are not easily reproduced in other, more traditional ways of working. Jean and Geoffrey Underwood argue that there is a case for *not* putting a computer on every child's desk in order to promote group work with IT, as 'the gains for cognitive development are demonstrable' (Underwood and Underwood, 1990, p. 168).

It would, however, be naive to assume that putting two or three children together with a computer in a corner will ensure an effective learning experience. Everyone has experienced situations where it is much easier to sit back rather than exert oneself and engage in the difficult task of thinking. There needs to be purpose, structure and challenge to encourage the children to develop the skills of discussion, negotiation and collaboration. Graham Peacock (1993) noted that giving children a word processor did not develop writing skills, and suggested that opportunities to highlight particular issues have to be exploited by the teacher, who is aware of the underlying intentions for cognitive development and for the task in hand.

NEW WAYS OF WORKING

At present, most of the attention has been given to the ways in which children interact with each other around the computer, working together *with* IT. There are many interesting possibilities raised by the developments in interacting *through* IT. Children can communicate with others remotely through a network, fax, electronic mail and computer conferencing, the last of which involves the contributions of several participants at once. The nature of the interaction can vary from formal to informal; the participants can retain a degree of anonymity and take time to consider and compose their responses.

IT has the potential to organize and process information, freeing the children to ask questions, look for answers, take risks in exploration and use a wide range of resources for information. They can develop a positive attitude to their work by using real and relevant data and presenting work in a polished and accessible form. A positive experience of IT in the classroom, developing children's confidence in working as individuals and with others, should contribute to the general quality of their learning.

The teachers' experience

THE VARIETY OF TEACHERS' ROLES

Teachers' experience of IT in the classroom is affected by a number of factors, some similar to the children's attitude to and experience of technology and some related more specifically to the teacher's role and expectations. The teacher's beliefs and values about the nature of education and schooling affect how life in the classroom is organized and managed, and the background experience of and attitude to new technology will also affect the role it plays in that classroom. If the teacher's experience is to be positive and encouraging, there needs to be some awareness of the challenges and frustrations of using IT in personal and professional work.

An IT capability for teachers was discussed in Chapter 1 (NCET, 1994a), and was said to include:

- basic technical competence;
- a positive attitude;
- an understanding of the education potential of IT;
- an ability to use it effectively in the curriculum;
- an ability to manage the resources in the classroom;
- an ability to evaluate its use in the children's learning.

It is interesting that most of these items of 'capability' refer to general teaching abilities of educational understanding and evaluation, which all teachers should strive to develop and refine throughout their teaching careers. The technical

149

competence acquired with new and changing resources is therefore developed in a meaningful context: that of evaluating resources to support children's learning, both in curriculum areas and in their IT capability.

It is important always to keep in mind the balance between technical and educational understanding. A key question, however, which teachers must ask themselves is, 'Does the presence of IT in our classroom affect my role and responsibilities as a teacher?' The inclusion of IT capability in the National Curriculum certainly affects the teacher's responsibilities, in that children are required to develop it through the curriculum, and there are clear indications that IT has the potential to support children's learning, cognitively and socially, in unique ways. The teacher's understanding of the processes involved in the nature of the interaction between children, new technology and teachers is crucial, in that it influences the variety of roles adopted and teaching strategies used to support the children's own understanding.

Knowing when to adopt appropriate teaching strategies in particular situations for children's different needs and interests is a challenge for teachers and lies at the heart of the reflection, evaluation and personal development that takes place throughout their careers. The awareness of one's *own* learning about the nature of children's learning becomes richer with time and experience, and it is difficult for inexperienced students and novice teachers to believe that they will ever acquire this; hence the many cries for 'tips for teachers' and 'just tell us how to *do* it' (Claxton, 1990).

The teacher can be seen as an instructor or demonstrator, a project manager, a consultant, a provider of resources, a questioner, an explainer, an observer and a co-learner. Supporting children in becoming more autonomous learners, able to think and find things out for themselves, is a tremendous responsibility, needing a subtle skill to balance the various roles and interactions. Children need guidance and support in order to 'taste the success that will encourage them to do better things' (Hill, 1990, p. 28), and an effective teacher will need to know when to 'build' and when to 'dismantle' 'scaffolds [to] help children to learn how to achieve heights that they cannot scale alone' (Wood, 1988, p.80).

It is knowing when and how to intervene to encourage pupil autonomy and contributions that influences the quality of the learning experience for both child and teacher. Knowing when to stand back in order to allow children time to work through uncertainty to solutions; knowing when to provide new information or skills to equip the children in their task; knowing when to ask a question to challenge or divert; knowing how to balance guidance and sharing of expertise with providing opportunities for children to think and work things out for themselves – such knowledge implies 'intelligent action' on behalf of the teacher. It is this intelligent action that lies at the heart of effective teaching skills, and which reflective teachers develop throughout their teaching careers (Wragg, 1993).

There is a variety of research evidence to indicate that teachers do in fact alter their roles and ways of working with IT, from shifting the management and control of the activity to the children and computer, to varying the nature of the interventions according to the technical experience and cognitive needs of the children (Fraser *et al.*, 1988; Olson, 1988; Hoyles and Sutherland, 1989). This requires careful thought, sensitivity and willingness to let go of confidence and competence whilst becoming familiar with new resources and working styles. It is also exciting and encouraging in identifying the distinctive roles and responsibilities of the teacher moving into the twenty-first century, instead of using new technology to reinforce the activities and methods of the classrooms of thirty years ago.

SUPPORTING THE TEACHERS' WORK

Teachers should also consider how IT can support their own personal and professional work. MAPE (Micros and Primary Education), a national association of primary schools and teachers, highlighted ways in which IT could enhance the quality of teachers' work and administration:

- Help to be better informed by providing access to vast amounts of information using CD ROM or network communications – from encyclopaedias to newspaper archives
- Save time by using IT applications to prepare and present work
- Help to support differentiation by enabling the creation, editing and development of materials to suit learners' needs

151

- Improve image by providing the opportunity to produce high quality materials from school brochures to CVs
- Improve efficiency by organizing and retrieving information, enabling rapid communications by electronic means and avoiding repetitive tasks from mail shots to worksheets
- Support creativity by enabling the manipulation and development of multimedia presentation of resources
- Help to bring teaching to life by providing the children access to a range of ways of interacting with information.

(MAPE, 1994, pp. 20–1)

The students' experience

PARTNERSHIP IN THE CLASSROOM

Practical, school-based experience for student teachers is very demanding in that students are expected to experience a wide range of classroom situations and teaching strategies. They need to develop their competence in planning, presentation, organization, management, evaluation, assessment, curriculum knowledge and work with colleagues and parents. They are also expected to develop their personal and professional IT capability in technical familiarity, educational understanding, organization of resources and groups of children, and observation and evaluation of the quality of children's experiences.

It is no wonder that students and mentors in schools find this a daunting prospect, particularly in a time of pressure and change in the content and assessment of the National Curriculum. Student teachers on initial education degree and postgraduate courses have a wide variety of previous experience and confidence with IT, and need carefully differentiated and subject-related courses in the higher education institutions. There is evidence that they are increasingly confident about their own IT skills, but have limited opportunity to develop IT capability in their school experience (Davis and Coles, 1993; Hodgkinson and Wild, 1994). This can be related to the lack of priority given to IT in a student's teaching practice by class teachers and mentors. As one mentor described it, 'IT is just another plate to spin!' (Loveless, in press). It has also been noted that student teachers focus more on the value of IT capability to the subject, than on the development of thinking skills (Dunn and Ridgway, 1994).

Although the picture may seem to have been presented in a gloomy light, there are considerable changes being made in the development of partnerships between schools and higher education institutions in providing appropriate experiences for students in order to meet the Department for Education and National Curriculum requirements. The National Council for Educational Technology emphasizes the need for continuing development in IT capability, from initial teacher training, through induction and on to in-service education (NCET, 1994a). A series of research projects in sixteen higher education institutions (HEI) was set up to investigate key issues in developing student IT confidence and strengthening links with partner schools through the use of IT (NCET, 1994d). The projects highlighted the need for close consultation and clear understanding of the distinct roles of the HEI and partner schools. For example, the HEI might be the appropriate place for students to develop both their technical capability and understanding of the educational rationale for using IT in learning and teaching, whereas the school might be a more appropriate place to consider issues of organization, management and evaluation, and to observe classroom practice. Attention was also drawn to the advantages of using electronic mail in providing immediate links between students and tutors and in building students' IT confidence, both in their own use of the resources and in the curriculum.

BUILDING STUDENTS' IT CAPABILITY

Student teachers need not 'blink in the headlights' of all these demands in the limited time available during a school experience. It is important to focus on key areas of planning and organization with IT, which can be observed and evaluated with small groups of children and developed as experience and confidence develop. At first it is wise to focus on an area of curriculum strength in which there is already some understanding of the knowledge, skills and concepts which form the framework for the activity.

Student IT capability	When?	What?	Which resources?	Where?	IT strand?	Comments
Basic technical capability						
use a range of IT resources and applications with confidence						
manage IT resources						
reflect on your own learning of IT skills						
Positive attitudes to IT and its place in education						
use at least one particular IT application with a high degree of mastery						
tackle new applications without hesitation						
assess the educational potential of new technologies						
Understanding of the educational potential of IT						
demonstrate an understanding of the way in which IT contributes to teaching and learning						
Ability to use IT effectively in the curriculum						
prepare schemes of work which integrate IT use						

Figure 7.1 A profile of the development of student IT capability.

154

Student IT capability	When?	What?	Which resources?	Where?	IT strand?	Comments
plan and deliver learning activities involving the selection and use of IT appropriate to age phase and NC subject						
justify the use of IT within a particular scheme or activity						
Manage IT in the classroom						
use IT effectively with a small group and in a normal classroom environment						
Evaluate IT use						
critically review a range of software and hardware						
evaluate their usefulness and appropriateness for pupils of different ages and abilities						
appraise your own use of IT						
Ensure differentiation and progression						
plan and implement a scheme of work appropriate for an individual pupil which incorporates the use of IT and modify as necessary						
effectively assess and record pupil achievement						

155

IT capability can be mapped on to the plans for a specific activity in which the timing, starting points, organization of groups, outcomes and follow-up are clearly related to the appropriate themes and resources. For example, an activity in looking at words, sequences and format in writing poetry could include a group of two or three children using a concept keyboard overlay or a word processing program with a word list to write their poems, whilst other groups use pencil and paper. The overlay and word list could be developed from the class introduction of a stimulus and discussion, and presented to the non-computer groups as a poster or display. It is not necessary for every child in the class to have the same experience in a limited time, as on a production line. The student teacher may learn more about children and IT by observing two or three groups using a word processor for different types of writing tasks, such as poems, letters and descriptions for classroom displays.

It is useful to keep a profile of the development of student IT capability, an example of which is given in Figure 7.1.

Such a profile enables students, mentors and tutors to identify where opportunities to develop IT capability have arisen, where experience has been developed, and where the areas for further attention and development lie. Evidence of the nature of the work with children and the development of evaluation and personal appraisal can be collected or cross-referenced to other working documents and school experience files built up over the course. It is essential that all teachers are aware of the need for continuing professional development from initial teacher training to induction and in-service, and such profiles assist in the reflection and planning necessary in professional growth.

What is important in the development of the student or novice teacher's understanding of children's IT capability is the observation and evaluation of the ways in which the children work on the task with the IT resources, and the demands that are made of the teacher in terms of technical support, interventions and questions. The focus should always be on the quality of the children's experience rather than the quantity of print outs achieved for the wall display!

Evaluating the classroom experience

Being observed, appraised and assessed by any visitor to the classroom is a nerve-racking experience, whether the visitor be a colleague, mentor, tutor or inspector, but it is important to identify the criteria by which standards of achievement and quality of learning by pupils are recognized. The NCET guide *Reviewing IT* defines clear quality indicators for review, based upon the OFSTED (1994) framework and the professional advice and guidance of IT advisers (NCET, 1994e). These indicators highlight issues relating to the children's attitude, confidence and awareness of appropriate IT use as well as their knowledge, skills, understanding and progression in IT capability. It is interesting to consider the criteria used in the two key areas – standards of achievement and quality of learning – and note the focus on the quality of the children's experience:

Standards of achievement:

1 Pupils demonstrate IT capability appropriate to their ability.
2 Pupils develop IT capability more or less evenly across the key aspects appropriate to the key stage.
3 Pupils are able to apply acquired skills and knowledge to new contexts successfully.
4 Pupils show an ability to judge when the use of IT has merits over other methods.
5 Pupils are able to select the most appropriate IT tool to use for tasks set.

Quality of learning:

1 Pupils show a greater willingness to pose questions because IT reduces the labour involved in answering them.
2 Pupils show a greater willingness to look for answers because IT makes information retrieval, data analysis and modelling easier.
3 Pupils show a greater willingness to take risks (in study and exploration) because unsatisfactory outcomes can be amended more easily.

4 Pupils use a broader range of resources and media because IT facilitates organization and retrieval, and is itself an information medium.

5 Pupils show an ability to learn and do by iteration rather than through one single attempt, because IT makes experimentation faster and easier.

6 Pupils show a more positive attitude to work because IT makes possible the capture/retrieval and analysis of real, relevant and up-to-date data, polished presentation and the designing and building of systems which perform real tasks.

7 Pupils collaborate on tasks to produce outcomes and use IT to facilitate such collaboration.

These criteria should not only act as indicators for inspection, but should inform and underpin the general principles of planning, policy and development of IT capability in the children's experience.

Postscript: today and tomorrow

The theme that has run throughout this book has been the importance of asking the question 'Why?' before 'How?' – of putting pedagogy before technology, and focusing on the quality of learning experiences. The emphasis has been on asking questions of and developing ideas with the technology available in classrooms today; but there also needs to be a vision of the possibilities for tomorrow. IT certainly has the potential for exciting and profound changes in education in terms of 'what' we learn, 'where' we learn and 'when' we learn. It can act as a catalyst in initiating new ways of learning, thinking and working for children and teachers. It can be seen as a medium through which learners and teachers can communicate, reflecting a view of learning in which human knowledge and thought develop through interaction, participation and communication. It has the potential for 'reorganizing instruction within the classroom and for making possible the extension of education beyond the classroom' (Cole and Griffin, 1987, p. 45).

Parents and teachers may express disquiet about the growing

influence of computer games, virtual reality and 'cybersurfing' in children's lives – often using the same phrases their parents and teachers used about watching TV or train spotting every weekend. Certainly, we should be concerned about the nature and underlying values of the material with which children interact, but we should also acknowledge the development of children's information-handling skills – observing, hypothesizing and testing – and participation with a range of new media.

There have been many initiatives and projects undertaken in recent years to evaluate the potential of new technologies for learning. CD ROM, portable computers, multimedia, electronic links between home and school, and the network of global communications have all given indications of the variety of ways and places in which IT can be used. Locations as diverse as community colleges and cyberspace cafés have been set up to provide access for groups ranging from the University of the Third Age to unemployed youths in the streets of Belfast. In Australia, children living in remote districts have been linked electronically with their schools and classmates, involving parents and teachers in providing support for their learning. In the USA, the National Information Infrastructure, or 'information superhighway', is the vision for providing information and communication in every home, public building and workplace, giving access to areas including research, home shopping, special interest conferences and personalized news services. In the UK, broadcasting, cable and communications companies are developing similar infrastructures, and the BBC Networking Club is evaluating schools' access to and use of the Internet.

The role of IT in our future is seen as utopia by some, dystopia by others. A society characterized by hackers, viruses, surveillance, isolation, automation and artificial, mechanistic images of 'human intelligence' may not appeal to many (Matthews, 1992). However, a society in which people are at ease with a complex, participatory environment which enables them to browse through and communicate information using a variety of media and forms of presentation can be more attractive. It can support a model of learning which reflects autonomy and interaction, exploration and collaboration, and develops the capability to choose when something is worth doing with IT and when it is not.

Teachers need not be seen only as 'information providers', but can be facilitators and guides, able to engage in higher-order interactions of questioning, explaining and challenging. Schools need not be seen as places for delivering the curriculum to groups of thirty disparate individuals, but perhaps can provide tutorial, social and specialist resources, from the arts to athletics. We must have an informed and critical view of the opportunities, constraints, bias and cultural values associated with the context in which learners use IT. 'Why?' and 'How?' need to be asked of the purpose and impact of IT in our children's future, just as much as they do of using the computer on the trolley in the corner of the classroom.

Keeping Up to Date

Information technology is a fast-changing field, in terms of the resources available and the ways in which they are being used in education. It is difficult to 'keep up' with all the new developments, but it is important to be aware of the direction of those developments and the implications they might have for teachers' work and practice. Below are some addresses and publications which may be useful in providing information, contacts and links with other interested colleagues.

Organizations
The National Council for Educational Technology (NCET)
Millburn Hill Road,
Science Park
Coventry
CV4 7JJ
Tel: 01203 416994
In addition to publications, seminars and exhibitions, NCET have a LINK-IT scheme, providing sources of local support.

Micros and Primary Education (MAPE)
A national association of primary teachers which publishes a journal (Micro-Scope), runs special editions and software offers, and presents local events and an annual national conference.
Subscriptions and membership:
Val Siviter
Cilgeraint Farm
St Ann's
Nr Bethesda
Gwynedd
LL57 4AX
Tel: 01248 602655
1995 rate: £15 p.a. (£10 p.a. student)

MAPE Micro-Scope Editor:
Chris Robinson
99 Foxcote
Wokingham
RG11 3PG
Tel: 01734 733718

Northwest SEMERC
A centre for the production and dissemination of IT resources
for learners with special educational needs.
Northwest SEMERC
Fitton Hill CDC
Rosary Road
Oldham
OL8 2QE
Tel: 0161 627 4469 and 0161 627 2381

Hardware manufacturers
Research Machines plc
New Mill House
183 Milton Park
Abingdon
Oxford
OX14 4SE

Acorn Computers Ltd
Acorn House
Vision Park
Histon
Cambridge
CB4 4AE

Apple Computers (UK) Ltd
6 Roundwood Avenue
Stockley Park
Uxbridge
UB1 11BB

Useful publications
Micro-Scope, the journal of MAPE (see above).

Educational Computing and Technology, a monthly journal on IT in schools.
1995 subscription rates: £20 p.a.
Jubilee House
The Oaks
Ruislip
Middlesex
HA4 7LF
Tel: 01895 622112

Times Educational Supplement, an IT resources page each week and a Computer Update at regular intervals.

Exhibitions and conferences
BETT, an annual exhibition in London for all producers of IT resources in education, from the large hardware manufacturers to cottage industry software (usually in January).

Resource, an annual conference and exhibition in Doncaster (usually in November).

Micros for Special Needs, an annual exhibition in Oldham of IT resources for special educational needs (usually in October).

MAPE Annual Conference, held at various venues around the UK, incorporating workshops, presentations and exhibitions (usually in March/April).

NCET LINK-IT, centres and local authority professional centres arrange exhibitions and conferences at regular intervals.

Bibliography

Alderson, G. (1992) Information handling and the development of statistical understanding in primary children, in Lodge, J. (ed.) (1992) *Computer Data Handling in the Primary School.* London: David Fulton in association with the Roehampton Institute, pp. 111–20.

Barbieri, M.S. and Light, P. (1992) Interaction, gender and performance on a computer-based problem solving task. *Learning and Instruction* 2, 199–214.

Bennett, N. and Dunne, E. (1992) *Managing Classroom Groups.* Hemel Hempstead: Simon and Schuster Education.

Bennett, N., Wragg, E.C., Carre, C.G. and Carter, D.S.G. (1992) A longitudinal study of primary teachers' perceived competence in, and concerns about, National Curriculum implementation. *Research Papers in Education* 7 (1), 53–78.

Beynon, J. (1993a) Technological literacy: where do we go from here? *Journal of Information Technology for Teacher Education* 2 (1), 7–35.

Beynon, J. (1993b) Computers, dominant boys and invisible girls; or 'Hannah, it's not a toaster, it's a computer!', in Beynon, J. and Mackay, H. (eds) (1993) *Computers into Classrooms: More Questions than Answers.* London and Washington, DC: Falmer Press, pp. 160–89.

Beynon, J. (1993c) Epilogue. Technological literacy: where do we all go from here?, in Beynon, J. and Mackay, H. (eds) (1993) *Computers into Classrooms: More Questions than Answers.* London and Washington, DC: Falmer Press, pp. 212–32.

Beynon, J. and Mackay, H. (eds) (1993) *Computers into Classrooms: More Questions than Answers.* London and Washington, DC: Falmer Press.

Blease, D. (1986) *Evaluating Educational Software.* London: Croom Helm.

Blease, D. and Cohen, L. (1990) *Coping with Computers.* London: Paul Chapman.

Blomeyer, R. (1993) A case study of microcomputers in art education, in Beynon, H. and Mackay, H. (eds) (1993) *Computers into Classrooms: More Questions than Answers*. London and Washington, DC: Falmer Press, pp. 39–77.

Brightman, A. (1989) Challenging the myth of disability. *Educom*, Winter.

Bruner, J. (1986) *Actual Minds, Possible Worlds*. Cambridge, MA, and London: Harvard University Press.

Carter, K. (1987) Data: Huddersfield Polytechnic, in Beynon, J. and Mackay, H. (eds) (1993) *Computers into Classrooms: More Questions than Answers*. London and Washington, DC: Falmer Press.

Cavendish, S. (1994) Spreadsheets, in Underwood, J (ed.) (1994) *Computer Based Learning: Potential into Practice*. London: David Fulton, pp. 102–15.

Chandler, D. (1984) *Young Learners and the Microcomputer*. Milton Keynes: Open University Press.

Chandler, D. (1990) The ideology of educational computing. *British Journal of Educational Technology* **21** (3), 165–74.

Chandler, D. and Marcus, S. (eds) (1985) *Computers and Literacy*. Milton Keynes: Open University Press.

Clark, M. (1985) Young writers and the computer, in Chandler, D. and Marcus, S. (eds) (1985) *Computers and Literacy*. Milton Keynes: Open University Press, pp. 12–25.

Claxton, G. (1984) *Live and Learn: An Introduction to the Psychology of Growth and Change in Everyday Life*. London: Harper and Row.

Claxton, G. (1990) *Teaching to Learn*. London: Cassell.

Clements, D.H. and Gullo, D.F. (1984) Effects of computer programming on young children's cognition. *Journal of Educational Psychology* **76**, 1051–8.

Cochran-Smith, M. and Lytle, S.L. (1993) *Inside/Outside: Teacher Research and Knowledge*. New York: Teachers' College Press.

Cockburn, C. (1988) Women and Technology: opportunity is not enough, in Jones, A. and Scrimshaw, P. (eds.) (1988) *Computers in Education 5–13*. Milton Keynes and Philadelphia: Open University Press, pp. 97–108.

Cole, M. and Griffin, P. (eds) (1987) *Contextual Factors in Education: Improving Science and Mathematics Education for Minorities and Women*. Madison, WI: Centre for Education Research.

Culley, L. (1988) Girls, boys and computers. *Educational Studies* **14**, 3–8.

Culley, L. (1993) Gender equity and computing in secondary schools: issues and strategies for teachers, in Beynon, J. and Mackay, H. (eds) (1993) *Computers into Classrooms: More Questions than Answers.* London and Washington, DC: Falmer Press, 147–59.

Daiute, C. (1985) *Writing and Computers.* Wokingham: Addison-Wesley.

Dalton, D.W. and Hannafin, M.J. (1987) The effects of word processing on written composition. *Journal of Educational Research* **80**, 338–42.

Davidson, J.I. (1989) *Children and Computers Together in the Early Childhood Classroom.* Albany, NY: Delmar.

Davis, N. and Coles, D. (1993) *Students' IT Experience and Related Data across the UK on Entry to Initial Teacher Training 1991–3.* Association for Information Technology in Teacher Education.

Davis, N. and Coles, D. (in press). Updated report on *Students' IT Experience and Related Data across the UK on Entry to Initial Teacher Training 1991–3.*

Dean, J. (1992) *Organising Learning in the Primary School Classroom* (second edition). London and New York: Routledge.

Dearing, R. (1994) *The National Curriculum and its Assessment: Final Report.* London: School Curriculum and Assessment Authority.

DES (1988) *National Curriculum: Task Group on Assessment and Testing: A Report.* London: DES/Welsh Office.

DES (1990) *Education Observed: Information Technology and Special Educational Needs in Schools.* London: HMSO

DES (1991) *A Survey of Information Technology in Schools.* London: Government Statistical Service.

DfE (1995) *Information Technology in the National Curriculum.* London: HMSO

Dodds, D. (1980) Blue Peter? Some aspects of model making in the primary classroom, in Wharry, D. (ed.) (1989) *Posing and Solving Problems with Control Technology: A Course Reader.* MicroElectronics Primary Project.

Donaldson, M. (1978) *Children's Minds.* London: Fontana.

Driscoll, M. (1987) Boats. *Computers in Primary Schools ILEA Newsletter* **14**, 10–17.

Dunn, S. and Morgan, V. (1987) *The Impact of the Computer on Education: A Course for Teachers.* London: Prentice Hall.

Dunn, S. and Ridgway, J. (1994) What CATE did: an exploration of the effects of the CATE criteria on students' use of information technology during teaching practice. *Journal of Information Technology for Teacher Education* **3**, (1), 39–50.

Eastman, S.T. and Krendl, K. (1987) Computers and gender: differential effects of electronic search on students' achievement and attitude. *Journal of Research and Development in Education* **20**, 41–8.

Evans, A. (1994) Don't believe your eyes. *Times Educational Supplement,* 5 August, 22.

Evans, C. (1980) *The Mighty Micro.* Philadelphia: Coronet.

Eyre, R. (1993) The Wiltshire Laptop Project. *Micro-Scope,* **40**.

Finlayson, H.M. (1984) The transfer of mathematical problem-solving skills from LOGO experience. *Research paper no. 238.* Edinburgh: Department of Artificial Intelligence, University of Edinburgh.

Finnegan, R., Salaman, G. and Thompson, K. (1987) *Information Technology: Social Issues.* Hodder and Stoughton in association with the Open University.

Fisher, E. (1993a) The teacher's role, in Scrimshaw, P. (ed.) (1993) *Language, Classrooms and Computers.* London and New York: Routledge, pp. 57–74.

Fisher, E. (1993b) Access to learning: problems and policies, in Scrimshaw, P. (ed.) (1993) *Language, Classrooms and Computers.* London and New York: Routledge, pp. 75–90.

Forester, T. and Morrison, P. (1990) *Computer Ethics: Cautionary Tales and Ethical Dilemmas in Computing.* Oxford: Blackwell.

Fraser, R., Burkhardt, H., Coupland, J., Phillips, R., Pimm, D. and Ridgway, J. (1988) Learning activities and classroom roles with and without the microcomputer, in Jones, A. and Scrimshaw P. (eds) (1988) *Computers in Education 5–13.* Milton Keynes and Philadelphia: Open University Press, pp. 203–29.

Freeman, D. and Levett, J. (1986) Quest – two curriculum projects: perspectives, practice and evidence. *Computers and Education* **10** (1), 55–9.

Galton, M. and Williamson, J. (1992) *Group Work in the Primary Classroom.* London and New York: Routledge.

Govier, H. (ed.) (1985) *Posing and Solving Problems with a Micro.* MEP.

Bibliography

Graves, D.H. (1983) *Writing – Teachers and Children at Work*. London: Heinemann.

Grieve, R. and Hughes, M. (eds) (1990) *Understanding Children*. Oxford: Blackwell.

Griffiths, M. (1988) Strong feelings about computers. *Women's Studies Internationl Forum* 11, 145–54.

Groundwater-Smith, S. and Crawford, K. (1992) Computer literacy and matters of equity. *Journal of Information Technology for Teacher Education* 1 (2), 215–29.

Guillaume, A.M. and Rudney, G.L. (1993) Student teachers' growth towards independence: an analysis of their changing concerns. *Teaching and Teacher Education* 9, 65–80.

Hall, J. and Rhodes, V. (1988) *Microcomputers in Primary Schools: Some Observations and Recommendations for Good Practice*. London: Educational Computing Unit, Centre for Educational Studies, King's College.

Harvey, B. (1984) Why LOGO?, in Yazdani, M. (ed.) (1984) *New Horizons in Educational Computing*. Chichester: Ellis Horwood, pp. 21–39.

Hawkridge, D. and Vincent, T. (1992) *Learning Difficulties and Computers*. London and Philadelphia: Jessica Kinglsey.

Heppell, S. (1993) Teacher education, learning and the information generation: the progression and evolution of educational computing against a background of change. *Journal of Information Technology for Teacher Education* 2 (2), 229–37.

Heppell, S. (1994) Multimedia and learning: normal children, normal lives and real change, in Underwood, J. (ed.) (1994) *Computer Based Learning: Potential into Practice*. London: David Fulton, pp. 152–61.

Hill, J. (1990) Children in control, *Teachers Voices* 2.

Hodgkinson, K. and Wild, P. (1994) Tracking the development of student information technology capability: IT in a primary postgraduate certificate of education course over three years. *Journal of Information Technology for Teacher Education* 3 (1), 101–14.

Hope, M. (ed.) (1986) *The Magic of the Micro – A Resource for Children with Learning Difficulties*. London: CET on behalf of MEP.

Howard, J. (1991) *Information Skills and the Secondary Curriculum: Some Practical Approaches*. Library and Information Research

Report 84. London: British Library Research and Development Department.

Howe, J.A.M., O'Shea, T. and Plane, F. (1979) Teaching mathematics through Logo programming: An evaluation study. *Proceedings of the International Federation for Information Processing Working Conference on Computer Assisted Learning.* London: IFIP.

Howe, J.A.M., Ross, P.M., Johnson, K.R. and Inglis, R. (1984) Model building, mathematics and Logo, in Yazdani, M. (ed.) (1984) *New Horizons in Educational Computing.* Chichester: Ellis Horwood, pp. 54–71.

Hoyles, C. (ed.) (1988) *Girls and Computers: General Issues and Case Studies of Logo in the Mathematics Classroom.* Bedford Way Papers 34. London: Institute of Education, University of London.

Hoyles, C. and Sutherland, R. (1989) *Logo Mathematics in the Classroom.* London: Routledge.

Hoyles, C., Sutherland, R. and Healey, I. (1990) *Children Talking in Computer Environments. New Insights on the Role of Discussion in Mathematics Learning,* in Durkin, K. and Shine, B. (eds) (1990) *Language and Mathematical Education.* Milton Keynes: Open University Press.

Hughes, M. (1990) Children's computation, in Grieve, R. and Hughes, M. (eds) (1990) *Understanding Children.* Oxford: Blackwell, pp. 121–39.

Hughes, M., Brackenbridge, A. and Macleod, H. (1987) Children's ideas about computers, in Rutkowska, J.C. and Crook, C. (eds) (1987) *Computers, Cognition and Development: Issues for Psychology and Education.* Chichester: John Wiley, pp. 9–34.

Hughes, M., Brackenbridge, A., Bibby, A. and Greenhough, P. (1988) Girls, boys and turtles: gender effects in young children learning with Logo, in Hoyles, C. (ed.) (1988) *Girls and Computers: General Issues and Case Studies of Logo in the Mathematics Classroom.* Bedford Way Papers 34. London: Institute of Education, University of London, 31–9.

Hunter, P. (1988) The writing process and word processing. *Micro-Scope Special: Writing,* 3–8.

Johnson, R., Johnson, D. and Stanne, M. (1986) Comparison of computer assisted cooperative, competitive and individualistic learning. *American Educational Research Journal* **23**, 382–92.

Johnson, R.T., Johnson, D.W. and Stanne, M.B. (1985) Effects of co-operative, competitive and individualistic goal structures on computer-assisted instruction. *Journal of Educational Psychology* **77**, 668–77.

Jones, A. and Scrimshaw, P. (eds) (1988) *Computers in Education 5–13*. Milton Keynes and Philadelphia: Open University Press.

Kelly, A.V. (ed.) (1984) *Microcomputers and the Curriculum*. London: Harper and Row.

Kemmis, S., Atkins, R. and Wright, E. (1977) *How do Students Learn?* Working Papers on Computer Assisted Learning, Occasional Paper 5. Norwich: Centre for Applied Research in Education, University of East Anglia.

Kirkup, G. and Keller, L.S. (eds) (1992) *Inventing Women: Science, Technology and Gender*. Cambridge: Polity Press in association with the Open University.

Klahr, D. and Carver, S.M. (1988) Cognitive objectives in a LOGO debugging curriculum: instruction, learning and transfer. *Cognitive Psychology* **20**, 362–404.

Kruger, A.C. (1993) Peer collaboration: conflict, co-operation or both? *Social Development* **2**, 165–82.

Labbett, B. (1988) Skilful neglect, in Schostak, J.F. (ed.) (1988) *Breaking into the Curriculum: The Impact of Information Technology on Schooling*. London and New York: Methuen, pp.89–104.

Littleton, K., Light, P., Barnes, P., Messer, D. and Joiner, R. (1993) Gender and software effects in computer-based problem solving. Paper presented at the Society for Research in Child Development, New Orleans, March.

Lodge, J. (ed.) (1992) *Computer Data Handling in the Primary School*. London: David Fulton in association with the Roehampton Institute.

Loveless, A.M. (1995) IT's another plate to spin: primary school mentors perceptions of supporting student experience of information technology in the classroom. *Journal of Information Technology for Teacher Education*, **4**(1), 39–50.

MAPE (1994) *Microscope Special: IT Starts Here!* Kettering: Newman College with MAPE/Castlefield.

Marland, M. (1981) *Information Skills in the Secondary Curriculum*. Schools Council Curriculum Bulletin 9. London: Methuen Educational.

Marland, M. (1991) Article in *Guardian*, 2 October.

Mathieson, K. (1993) *Children's Art and the Computer.* Sevenoaks: Hodder and Stoughton.

Matthews, B. (1992) Towards an understanding of the social issues in information technology: concerning computers, intelligence and education. *Journal of Information Technology for Teacher Education* 1 (2), 201–13.

Maxwell, B. (1984) Why Logo?, in Kelly, A.V. (ed.) (1984) *Microcomputers and the Curriculum.* London: Harper and Row, pp. 84–106.

McKeown, S. (1994) When seeing is believing. *Times Educational Supplement,* 22 July, 30.

McTaggart, M. (1994) The art of seeing. Computer update, *Times Educational Supplement,* 25 March, 18.

Mercer, N. (1993) Computer-based activities in classroom contexts, in Scrimshaw, P. (ed.) (1993) *Language, Classroom and Computers.* London and New York: Routledge, pp. 27–39.

Moyles, J. (1992) *Organizing for Learning in the Primary Classroom: A Balanced Approach to Classroom Management.* Buckingham and Philadelphia: Open University Press.

NCC (1990) *Non-Statutory Guidance: Information Technology Capability.* York: NCC.

NCET (1990) *Information Skills and the National Curriculum: A Summary Sheet.* Coventry: NCET

NCET (1991a) *The IT Needs of Hearing-impaired Pupils and their Teachers.* Information Sheets 1 and 2. Coventry: NCET.

NCET (1991b) *On-line: Electronic Mail in the Curriculum.* Coventry: NCET.

NCET (1992a) *IT Support for Specific Learning Difficulties.* Coventry: NCET.

NCET (1992b) *IT and Students with Emotional and Behavioural Difficulties.* Coventry: NCET.

NCET (1994a) *Training Tomorrow's Teachers in Information Technology.* Coventry: NCET.

NCET (1994b) *Getting Started with Information Handling.* Coventry: NCET.

NCET (1994c) *Why Me? Why IT?* Coventry: NCET.

NCET (1994d) *Partnership in Initial Teacher Training.* Coventry: NCET.

NCET (1994e) *Reviewing IT.* Coventry: NCET.

Newton P. and Beck, E. (1993) Computing: an ideal occupation for women?, in Beynon, J. and Mackay H. (eds) (1993) *Computers into Classrooms: More Questions than Answers*. London and Washington, DC: Falmer Press, pp.130–46.

Noss, R. (1983) Doing maths while learning Logo. *Mathematics Teaching* **104**, 5–10.

OFSTED (1994) *Handbook for the Inspection of Schools*. London: HMSO.

Olson, J. (1988) *School Worlds – Microworlds; Computers and the Culture of the Classroom*. Oxford: Pergamon.

Owston, R.D. (1993) Computers and the teaching of writing: implications for teacher development. *Journal of Information Technology for Teacher Education* **2**(2), 239–50.

Papert, S. (1980) *Mindstorms*. Brighton: Harvester Press.

Papert, S. (1993) *The Children's Machine: Rethinking School in the Age of the Computer*. New York, London, Toronto, Sydney, Tokyo and Singapore: Harvester Wheatsheaf.

Pea, R.D. (1983) Logo programming and problem solving, in *Symposium: Chameleon in the Classroom: Developing Roles for Computers*. Technical Report 22. Center for Children and Technology, Bank Street College of Education, pp. 25–33.

Peacock, G. (1993) Word-processors and collaborative writing, in Beynon, J. and Mackay, H. (eds) (1993) *Computers into Classrooms: More Questions than Answers*. London and Washington, DC: Falmer Press, pp. 92–7.

Picasso, P. (1923) Picasso speaks. *The Arts (New York)*, May 315–26. Reprinted in Chipp, H.B. (1975) *Theories of Modern Art*. Berkeley, Los Angeles and London: University of California Press, p. 264.

Pollard, A. and Tann, S. (1993) *Reflective Teaching in the Primary School*. London: Cassell.

Rahamim, L. (1993) *Access to Word and Images*. Coventry: NCET/CENMAC.

Robinson, B. (1993) Communicating through computers in the classroom, in Scrimshaw, P. (ed.) (1993) *Language, Classroom and Computers*. London and New York: Routledge, pp. 111–29.

Ross, A. (1984a) *Making Connections*. London: Council for Educational Technology.

Ross, A. (1984b) Learning why to hypothesize: a case study of data processing in a primary school classroom, in Kelly, A.V. (ed.) (1984) *Microcomputers and the Curriculum*. London: Harper and Row, pp. 64–83.

Rutkowska, J.C. and Crook, C. (eds) (1987) *Computers, Cognition and Development: Issues for Psychology and Education.* Chichester: John Wiley.

Saloman, G. (1992) Studying the flute and the orchestra: controlled vs classroom research on computers. *International Journal of Educational Research* 14, 526–31.

Scaife, J. and Wellington, J. (1993) *Information Technology in Science and Technology Education.* Buckingham and Philadelphia: Open University Press.

Scanlon, E. and O'Shea, T. (eds) (1987) *Educational Computing.* Chichester: Open University Press and John Wiley.

Schostak, J.F. (ed.) (1988) *Breaking into the Curriculum: The Impact of Information Technology on Schooling.* London and New York: Methuen.

Scrimshaw, P. (1988) Computers in art education: threat or promise?, in Jones, A. and Scrimshaw, P. (eds) (1988) *Computers in Education 5–13.* Milton Keynes and Philadelphia: Open University Press, pp. 128–33.

Scrimshaw, P. (ed.) (1993) *Language, classrooms and computers.* London and New York: Routledge.

Senior, S. (1990) *Using IT across the National Curriculum.* Tunstall: Owlet Books.

Sharples, M. (1988) The use of computers to aid the teaching of creative writing, in Jones, A. and Scrimshaw, P. (eds.) (1988) *Computers in Education 5–13.* Milton Keynes and Philadelphia: Open University Press, pp. 134–46.

Sheingold, K., Hawkins, J. and Char, C. (1984) 'I'm the thinkist, you're the typist': the interaction of technology and the social life of classrooms. *Journal of Social Issues* 40(3), 49–61.

Siann, G., Durndell, A., Macleod, H. and Glissov, P. (1988) Stereotyping in relation to the gender gap in participation in computing. *Educational Research* 30, 98–103.

Simon, T. (1987) Claims for Logo: what should we believe and why?, in Rutkowska, J.C. and Crook, C. (eds) (1987) *Computers, Cognition and Development: Issues for Psychology and Education.* Chichester: John Wiley, pp. 115–33.

Smith, B. (1993) Laptops: the perfect writing tool? *Micro-Scope* 38, 22–3.

Somekh, B. (1988) Micro reflections. Paper delivered to BERA symposium on IT/Education, University of East Anglia, September.

Southall, R. (1992) The world of data handling and its place in primary education, in Lodge, J. (ed.) (1992) *Computer Data Handling in the Primary School.* London: David Fulton in association with the Roehampton Institute, pp. 1–18.

Stonier, T. and Conlin, C. (1985) *The Three Cs; Children, Computers and Communication.* Chichester: John Wiley.

Stradling, B., Sims, D. and Jamison, J. (1994) *Portable Computers Evaluation Summary.* Coventry: NCET.

Straker, A. (1985) Thinking things out: solving problems with a micro, in Govier, H. (ed.) (1985) *Posing and Solving Problems with a Micro.* MEP, pp. 8–16.

Straker, A. (1989) *Children using Computers.* Oxford: Blackwell.

Toffler, A. (1981) *The Third Wave.* London: Usborne.

Turkle, S. (1984) *The Second Self: Computers and the Human Spirit.* New York: Simon and Schuster.

Turkle, S. and Papert, S. (1990) Epistemological pluralism: styles and voices within the computer culture. *Signs: Journal of Women in Culture and Society* **16** (1).

Underwood, G. (1994) Collaboration and problem solving: Gender differences and the quality of discussion, in Underwood, J. (ed.) (1994) *Computer Based Learning: Potential into Practice.* London: David Fulton.

Underwood, G., Jindal, N. and Underwood, J. (1994) Gender differences and effects of cooperation in a computer-based language task. *Educational Research* **36**, 63–74.

Underwood, G., Underwood, J. and Turner, M. (1993) Children's thinking during collaborative computer-based problem solving. *Educational Psychology* **13**, 345–57.

Underwood, J. (1986) The role of the computer in developing children's classificatory abilities. *Computers in Education* **10** (1), 175–80.

Underwood, J. (ed.) (1994) *Computer Based Learning: Potential into Practice.* London: David Fulton.

Underwood, J. and Underwood, G. (1990) *Computers and Learning: Helping Children Acquire Thinking Skills.* Oxford: Blackwell.

Vygotsky, L.S. (1978) *Mind in Society.* Cambridge, MA: MIT Press.

Watson, D.M. (1987) *Developing CAL: Computers in the Curriculum.* London: Harper and Row.

Watson, D.M. (ed.) (1993) *The ImpacT Report: An Evaluation of the Impact of Information Technology on Children's Achievements in Primary and Secondary Schools.* London: Centre for Educational Studies, Kings College.

Weizenbaum, J. (1984) *Computer Power and Human Reason: From Judgment to Calculation.* London: Penguin.

Wellburn, E., Francis, L., Riecken, T. and Farragher, P. (1993) Changing roles: technology, staff development and action research at a Canadian middle school. *Journal of Information Technology for Teacher Education* **2** (2), 155–65.

Wellington, J.J. (1985) *Children, Computers and the Curriculum.* London: Harper and Row.

Whalley, P. (1992) Making control technology work in the classroom. *British Journal of Educational Technology,* **23** (3), 212–21.

Whalley, P. (1994) Control technology, in Underwood, J. (ed.) (1994) *Computer Based Learning: Potential into Practice.* London: David Fulton, pp. 137–51.

Wharry, D. (ed.) (1989) *Posing and Solving Problems with Control Technology: A Course Reader.* MEP.

Williams, N. and Holt, P. (eds) (1989) *Computers and Writing.* Oxford: Blackwell Scientific.

Wood, D. (1988) *How Children Think and Learn.* Oxford: Blackwell.

Woods, R.G. and Barrow, R. St C. (1988) Creativity, in Jones, A. and Scrimshaw, P. (eds) (1988) *Computers in Education 5–13.* Milton Keynes and Philadelphia: Open University Press, pp. 11–17.

Woolley, B. (1993) *Virtual Worlds.* London: Penguin.

Wragg, E.C. (1993) *Primary Teaching Skills.* London and New York: Routledge.

Yazdani, M. (ed.) (1984) *New Horizons in Educational Computing.* Chichester: Ellis Horwood.

Yazdani, M. (1989) Computational story writing, in Williams, N. and Holt, P. (eds) (1989) *Computers and Writing.* Oxford: Blackwell Scientific.

Name Index

Alderson, G.   55
Atkins, R.   17

Barbieri, M. S.   113
Barnes, P.   113
Barrow, R. St C.   41
Beck, E.   104, 105, 108, 109
Bennett, N.   2, 146
Beynon, J.   38, 107, 109, 143
Bibby, A.   112
Blease, D.   129
Brackenbridge, A.   21, 112
Brightman, A.   93
Bruner, J.   19, 70
Burkhardt, H.   20, 151
Burroughs, W.   35
Bush, Vannevar   35

Carre, C. G.   2
Carter, D. S .G.   2
Carter, K.   108
Carver, S. M.   89
Cavendish, S.   64
Chandler, D.   33, 37
Char, C.   147
Clark, M.   27
Claxton, G.   12, 150
Clements, D. H.   89
Cole, M.   158
Coles, D.   2, 104, 152
Coupland, J.   20, 151
Crawford, K.   108
Culley, l.   104, 105, 106, 108

Daiute, C.   31
Davis, N.   2, 104, 152
Dean, J.   146
Dearing, R.   131
DES   102, 116
DfE   15, 131
Donaldson, M.   70
Driscoll, M.   61
Dunn, S.   153
Dunne, E.   146

Eastman, S. T.   105
Evans, A.   49
Eyre, R.   33

Farragher, P.   20
Finlayson, H. M.   89
Fisher, E.   20, 116
Forester, T.   4
Francis, L.   20
Fraser, R.   20, 151
Freeman, D.   52, 56
Fox School,   61

Galton, M.   146
Greenhough, P.   112
Grieve, R.   70
Griffin, P.   158
Griffiths, M.   105
Groundwater-Smith, S.   108
Gullo, D. F.   89

Hall, J.   107
Harvey, B.   83
Hawkins, J.   147
Hawkridge, D.   93, 97, 99
Healey, I.   147
Heppell, S.   143
Hodgkinson, K.   152
Howe, J. A. M.   90
Hoyles, C.   20, 90, 103, 109, 111, 111, 113, 147, 151
Hughes, M.   21, 70, 113, 148
Hunter, P.   25, 26

Jamison, J.   34
Jindal, N.   114
Johnson, D.   147
Johnson, R.   147
Joiner, R.   113

Keller, L. S.   102, 104
Kelley, A. V.
Kemmis, S.   17
Kirkup, G.   102, 104
Klahr, D.   89
Krendl, K.   105
Kruger, A. C.   114

Labbett, B.   79
Levett, J.   52, 56
Light, P.   113
Littleton, K.   113

Loveless, A. M. 152

Mackay, H. 143
McKeown, S. 97
Macleod, H. 21
McTaggart, M. 95
MAPE 151, 152
Marland, M. 51, 54
Mathieson, K. 41, 47
Matthews, B. 5, 159
Maxwell, B. 88
Mercer, N. 20
Messer, D. 113
Morrison, P. 4
Moyles, J. 146

National Curriculum Council 11
NCET 14, 52, 95, 100, 101, 106,
    137, 149, 153, 157
Newton, P. 104, 105, 108, 109
North London Language
    Consortium 133, 134
Noss, R. 85

O'Shea, T. 90
OFSTED 136, 157
Olson, J. 19, 151
Owston, R. D. 38

Papert, S. 26, 72, 82, 84, 111–12,
    144
Pea, R. D. 89
Peacock, G. 38, 40, 148
Phillips, R. 20, 151
Piaget, J. 70, 84
Picasso, P. 50
Pimm, D. 20, 151
Plane, F. 90
Pollard, A. 146

Rahamim, L. 95
Rhodes, V. 107
Ridgway, J. 20, 151, 152
Riecken, T. 20

Ross, A. 54, 56

Scaife, J. 72, 74, 82
Scrimshaw, P. 33, 42, 46
Sharples, M. 37
Sheingold, J. 147
Simon, T. 89
Sims, D. 34
Smith, B. 29
Somekh, B. 104, 105
Southall, R. 52, 54, 56
Stanne, M. 147
Stradling, B. 34
Straker, A. 80, 88
Sutherland, R. 20, 90, 147, 151

Tann, S. 146
Toffler, A. 3
Turkle, S. 5, 75, 111–12
Turner, M. 114

Underwood, G. 1, 56, 72, 89, 104,
    112, 114, 147, 148
Underwood, J. 1, 56, 57, 65, 67–8,
    72, 89, 104, 112, 113, 114, 147,
    148

Vincent, T. 93, 97, 99
Vygotsky, L. S. 19, 70

Watson, D. M. 6, 22, 143
Weizenbaum, J. 75
Wellburn, E. 20
Wellington, J. 72, 74, 82, 129
Whalley, P. 79
Wild, P. 152
Williamson, J. 146
Wood, D. 70, 150
Woods, R. G. 41
Woolley, B. 35
Wragg, E. C. 151
Wright, E. 17

Yazdani, M. 37

Subject Index

access   4, 8, 65, 68, 72, 92, 93, 103, 107, 114, 116, 143
adventure games   35, 72–4, 91
animation   49
applications and effects   21
approaches to working   110–14
art education   41, 48
artificial intelligence   4, 5, 37, 84
assessment   133, 135, 137–40
attitudes   1, 12, 103, 104, 105–10, 145, 149, 158
authoring packages   36

bilingual pupils   115

CD ROM   16, 49, 63, 65, 68, 72, 96, 98, 115–16, 124, 159
census material   61–3
classification   56, 57, 58
clip art   43, 45
cognitive learning difficulties   97–100
cognitive skills   72, 89
collaboration   32–3, 39, 78, 79, 113, 116, 146, 148
communicating and handling information   15
communicating information   16, 23–4
communication   4, 50, 70, 105, 148, 158
composition   37, 38, 50
Computer Assisted Learning (CAL)   17
computer games   106, 159
computer skills   11
concept keyboard   64, 94, 97, 99, 124
confidence   1, 12–13, 21, 100, 101, 107, 117, 145
conjectural paradigm   17, 71, 89, 90
connections   63, 65, 68
constructivism   70
control technology   16, 69, 76–80, 91, 125
controlling, monitoring and modelling   15
cooperation   147
culture   4, 70, 84, 92, 106, 114
curriculum planning   131

databases   57–62
   binary trees   58–9
   flat file   60–63
   free text   59–60
   relational   63
datalogging   80–83, 122
Dearing Report   131
debugging   85, 89
desktop publisher   26, 32
digitizing   48
distancing   147
dyslexia   29, 100

editing   27, 29, 31, 39
electronic communications   26, 33, 159
eledtronic mail   33, 96, 148
emancipatory paradigm   18, 30
emergent capabilities   143
emotional and behavioural difficulties   100
experience of IT
   children   144–9
   students 152–7
   teachers   149–52

fair tests   60, 61
fax   97
fractal geometry   49

gender   79, 84, 92, 102–14, 117
graphics   42–6, 95, 98
graphs   81
group work   79, 112–14, 146–8

groups
    mixed sex 112, 113, 116
    single sex 112, 113, 114, 116

hardware 121
hearing impairment 96
home computers 105, 107, 116
hypertext 19, 26, 35-6
hypothesis testing 55, 56, 62-3, 68,
    82

images of IT 4-6, 105, 117
ImpacT Report 22, 143
information handling 51-68
information handling software 57
information society 53, 143
information superhighway 159
information
    analysis 53, 56, 81
    collection 54, 57, 81
    communication 56
    interpretation 67, 82, 83
    manipulation 56, 57
    organization 57, 68
    presentation 8, 32, 42, 53, 68, 81
    representation 57
    retrieval 8, 56, 65
    skills 51-4, 68
    storage 7, 56, 65
instructional paradigm 17
interaction 7, 38, 54, 70, 84, 90, 94,
    111, 112, 148
interactive video 73
interface 76
IT capability 10-14, 15, 21, 68, 116,
    130-36, 149, 153, 156, 157
IT in the National Curriculum
    15-17

jargon 106

keyboard skills 28
keywords 59

learning 2, 6, 7, 9, 19, 22, 54, 69, 70,
    83, 84, 88, 91, 144, 146, 150, 158,
    160
learning styles 110-11
learning paradigms 17

Memex machine 35
mental models 21, 65-6, 70, 84
microworlds 91
modelling 9, 16, 50, 69, 72-6
monitoring 16, 69, 80-83, 91, 125
multimedia 24, 32, 49, 72, 98, 159

National Curriculum 14, 69, 92,
    103, 130
National Gallery 49
networks 68, 73

OFSTED 136, 157

painting and drawing 43-4
physical disabilities 93-7
Pip 77, 87, 124
planning 130-36
portable computers 33, 81, 122, 159
presentation 39, 135
primitives 85, 87
problem solving 69, 71, 72, 77, 79,
    83, 89, 90, 112, 148
procedures 85, 87

quality of learning 157

representation 73, 75, 82
resources 119-30
revelatory paradigm 17, 71
reviewing 136
Reviewing IT 137, 157
Roamer 77, 87, 124

scanning 43, 45
sensory impairment 93-7
sensors 79, 80
simulations 72, 74-5
society 3, 4, 73, 102, 159
socio-cultural learning theories 70
socio-economic class 92, 114-15
software 119
software evaluation 129
Special Educational Needs 92-101
spelling checker 27, 29, 100
spirit of enquiry 55
spreadsheets 64, 75-6
standards of achievement 157

Subject Index

statistics 55
switches 95

talking books 95, 97
teacher training partnerships 151
teaching
 intervention 20, 90, 114, 151
 IT capability 13
 roles 19, 22, 30, 38, 79, 83, 90, 91,
  106, 117, 143, 149–51, 160
 strategies 150
technological literacy 6, 143
technological revolution 3, 4
thinking skills 56
Touch Explorer 64
transformation 45–6, 49, 50
turtle
 floor 77, 87
 screen 78, 87

videophone 97
virtual reality 9, 73, 74, 159
visual art 40–50
visual impairments 95
Vygotsky 19, 70

wordprocessor 26, 32, 98
 multilingual 26, 115
 talking 29, 95
writing 24–40
 audience 32
 composing and redrafting 30
 process 25